LET'S NA...
10,000 Boat Names

An Ingenious, Humorous, and
Authentic Source
for Beginners and Old Salts Alike.

by
John Corcoran and Lew Hackler

Illustrated by Bobby Basnight

Under the Editorship of
Patricia Rychlik Blaszak

SEVEN SEAS PRESS
Camden, Maine

Published by
Seascape Enterprises
P.O. Box 176
Colonial Heights, Virginia 23834

Fourth Printing, December 1992
Distributed by International Marine Publishing Company
Route 1, P.O. Box 220
Camden, Maine 04843
207-236-4837

"How is Hennery gettin' along with school, Charlly?"

"Not so well, Garge. They're learning him to spell taters with a 'p'."

INTRODUCTION

What's in a name? A lot, say the authors of this book.

Modern psychology would agree that the time and energy we invest in naming people, things, or boats, can often give clues into the personality, lifestyles, and values of the people doing the naming.

—John T. Thios, Associate Professor of Psychology,
*Richard Bland College of The College of William
and Mary; and sailor.*

ACKNOWLEDGEMENTS

Often, projects that appear simple at the onset become complicated as we get into them. This little book is no exception, as it began as a simple collection of boat names with no definitions. Few would have been interested in such a book.

As a larger, more complex idea evolved, it became apparent that most of what we are, and do, grows from our experiences, from our friends, and from our associations. Fond memories flowed through our minds as we recalled boats and experiences we shared. You know who you are out there, "Thanks again!".

Others who helped in a big way include our Editor, Pat Blaszak and our hawkeye proofreaders, Jean and Dick Betton. The cover was designed by Mark Smith of Creative Services, a sailor; and our many special typesetting needs were done by Sandy Adams of Typographics, also a sailor. We also thank Henry Wagner of Sailors Bookshelf, for his advice, and support. Most of the boating publications contributed to the lists unknowingly, but direct contribution came from Linda Horgan of Chesapeake Bay Magazine.

Many of the clubs we cruised and raced with will recognize many of their boats' names. These include Carolina Yacht Club, Seven Seas Cruising Association, Chesapeake Yacht Racing Association, Cruising Club of Virginia, Hopewell Yacht Club, Hunter Sailing Club, Stingray Harbor Yacht Club, and Jordon Point Yacht Club.

Most of all, thanks to Janice, my love and dearest critic, and all those creative, romantic, and mischievous boaters that dot the waterways of the world, without whom this book wouldn't exist.

CONTENTS

EDITOR'S NOTE:
Normal rules for alphabetical listing of names were not used because of the "poetic license" used in naming boats. Words are frequently mis(s)pelled intentionally, or combined or separated to suit the user, therefore a literal alphabetical listing was indicated.

1

A Witch's Brew:

Early Traditions & Superstitions

Throughout history, feminine names have often been selected for boats. In addition, large wooden ships were adorned with elaborately carved and painted female figureheads at the bow sprit. Many of these feminine images are still evident in maritime museums and seafood restaurants.

Ancient superstition held that bad luck would befall a ship or vessel which had its name changed. In modern times names are frequently changed as ownership passes from one owner to another.

# #

2 BROTHERS
2 EASY
3 CHEERS
3 TIMES A LADY
4 SEASONS
5 & 10
5TH AVE.
8-BALL
8 DAYS A WEEK
9 TO 5
"10"
"11"
11TH HOUR
11TH NIGHT
16 CANDLES
16 TONS
19TH NERVOUS
  BREAKDOWN

21 GUN SALUTE
26 MILES
38 SPECIAL
42ND STREET
49ER
50 WAYS
96 TEARS
99 LUFTBALLONS
1776
2001

A

A APPLE
AARDVARK
ABALONE
ABBEYDALE
ABBOTSFORD
ABC's

ABERCROMBIE
ABE'S LINCOLN
ABILITY
ABIQUIO
ABLE LADY
ABORIGINE
ABRACADABRA
ABSINTHE
ABSOLUTE _____
ABSOLUTE HAPPINESS
ABUNDANCE
ABUNDANT LIFE
ACADEMY HILL
ACADIA
ACAJOU
ACANTHUS
A CAPELLA
ACCENT
ACCIPITATE
ACCOLADE
ACCOMPLICE

ACCORD
ACCOUNTESS
ACE
ACE HIGH
ACE OF SPADES
ACE OF WANDS
ACES HIGH
ACEY
ACHES AND PAINS
ACHIEVEMENT
ACHIEVER
ACHILLEIOS
ACHILLE'S HEEL
ACKWITAL
A'COMPTE
ACORN
ACQUAINTANCE
ACQUIESCE
ACQUITTAL
ACQUITTED

ADIOS AMIGO
ADIRONDACK
_____ADJUSTER
ADJUSTER
AD LIB
ADMIRABLE
A DOGS LIFE
ADONIS
ADORABLE
ADMIRAL
ADRENALIN
ADRENAYN
ADRIA
ADRIATIC
ADRINA
ADVANCE
ADVANTAGE
AD VENTURE
ADVENTURE
_____ADVENTURE

AFFECTION
AFFECTIONATE
AFFECTIONIST
AFFIRMED
AFFLUENCE
AFFLUENT
AFLOAT
AFRICAN QUEEN
AFTER ALL
AFTER FIVE
AFTER FOUR
AFTERGLOW
AFTER HOURS
AFTERMATH
AFTERNOON DELIGHT
AFTER YOU
AGAIN
AGAIN & AGAIN
AGAINST ALL ODDS
AGAPE

The gods and goddesses of mythology continue to be called on, appropriately, for use as names of sea vessels, spaceships, and modern weapons: ACHILLE'S HEEL, AMPHITRITE, APHRODITE, APOLLO, ARGONAUT, ATHENA, ATLAS, ELECTRA, EOS, FLORÀ, FORTUNA, FREYA, HERCULES, ISIS, JASON, MERCURY, NEMESIS, NEPENTHE, NEPTUNE, OLYMPIC, PHAETHON, SATURN, UNICORN, VALKIRIE, VANADIS, and VENUS. Also, NECTAR O' GODS, and AMBROSIA, or food for the gods have been used.

ACROBAT
ACROPOLIS
ACRUX
ACT I
ACTIVATION
ACTIVE
ACT ONE
ACT_____
ACTION TOY
ACUPULCO GOLD
ADAGIO
ADAGO
ADAMANT
ADAM'S APPLE
AD ASTRA
ADD IN
ADEPT
ADHARA
ADIEU
ADIOS

ADVENTURER
ADVENTURIER
ADVENTURES
ADVENTURESS
ADVENTURE SEEKER
ADVENTUROUS
ADVOCATE
AEBI
AEGIS
AENA
AEOLUS
AERIE
AEROLUFF
AERONAUT
AERONUT
AEROSHIP
AEROSLED
_____AFFAIR
AFFAIR D'AMOUR
AFFAIRE D'OR

AGATE
AGEING DREAM
AGENDA
AGENT
AGENT ORANGE
AGGIE
AGGRESSIVE
AGGRESSOR
AGLOW
A GOGO
AGONY
AGUSTA
AHAB
AH SO
AIDA
AIKIDO
AIMWELL
AIRBORNE
AIRBUS
AIRCO

AIR CONDITION
AIRDALE
AIREL
AIRES
AIR EXPRESS
AIRFARE
AIRFOIL
AIRFORCE
AIRHORN
AIR MAIL
AIRMAIL
AIRONAUTICAL
AIRPLANE
AIRUS
AIRWAYS
AIRY
AJA
AJAX
AKAMAI
AKEAKAMAI

ALBA
ALBACORE
ALBAR
ALBATROSS
ALBATROSSI
ALBEMARLE
ALBEMARLE PIPPIN
ALBERT
ALCES
ALCHEMIST
ALCHEMY
ALCYONE
ALDEDO
ALDER
ALDORA
ALECTO
ALERT
ALETHEA
ALEXIS
ALFA

ALLEGHENY
ALLEGHENY MOON
ALLEGIANCE
ALLEGRO
ALLEY CAT
ALLEY OOP
ALLEZ CAT
ALL HEART
ALLHERS
ALLIANCE
ALL NIGHT LONG
ALL NINE
ALLOBAR
ALL OF US
ALLONS
ALL SHOOK UP
ALL THAT GLITTERS
ALL THE WAY
ALLURA
ALLURE

> *Names of famous barks, clipper ships and other windjammers, may spark interest, and hold special meaning for the owner: ARIEL, ATLANTIC, CONTEST, CORSAIR, CUTTY SARK, EAGLE, ESMERALDA, FLYING CLOUD, GATHERER, JAVA, LIGHTENING, LINDO, MARQUES, NORTHERN LIGHT, OLYMPIA, PHANTOM, PINAFORE, SEA NYMPH, SNOW SQUALL, TAEPING, and THERMOPYLAE.*

AKKA
AKVAVIT
ALABAMA
ALABAMA _____
ALABAMA JUBILEE
A LA CARTE
ALACRITY
ALADDIN
ALAMANCE
ALAMAR
A LA MODE
ALAMODE
ALAN
ALANA
ALARIC
ALARIS
ALARM
ALAS
ALASKA
A LASS
ALASTOR

AL FRESCO
ALGONQUIN
ALIAS
ALI-BABA
ALIBI
ALICE
ALICE TOO
ALICIA
ALIDA
ALIDIA
ALIEN
ALIEN 8
ALIENATOR
ALIMONY
ALIOTH
ALKAID
AL KUMAIT
ALL ABOARD
ALLAMANDA
ALL AMERICAN
ALL CHIEFS

ALLUREMENT
ALLURING
ALLUSION
ALLUSIVE
ALMA
ALMOST
ALMOST HEAVEN
AL NA'IR
ALO ALO
ALOBAR
ALOE
ALOHA
ALOFT
ALPHA
ALPHA & OMEGA
ALPHARD
ALPHECCA
ALPHORA
AL RIYADH
ALTAIR
ALTERED STATES

ALTERNATIVE
ALTHEA
ALTURA
ALUMBUS
ALUVA
ALVA
ALVENA
ALWAYS
ALWAYS ELEGANT
ALWAYS READY
ALWAYS TRUE
ALWAYS _____
AMAAMA
AMADEUS
AMADON LIGHT
AMAL
AMAL MARAMU
AMANDA
AMANTE
AMASEK

AMERICAN CLASSIC
AMERICAN CHARM
AMERICAN DREAM
AMERICAN EXPRESS
AMERICAN FLAG
AMERICAN HERITAGE
AMERICAN LEGION
AMERICAN MAJESTY
AMERICAN MARINER
AMERICAN PATRIOT
AMERICAN PIE
AMERICAN PRIDE
AMERICAN SAILOR
AMERICAN SALVOR
AMERICAN SEAMAN
AMERICAN SPIRIT
AMERICAN SPLENDOR
AMERICAN
  TRADITION
AMERICAN _____

ANDOVER
ANDRADE
ANDREA
ANDREA DORIA
ANDREANA
ANDROMEDA
AND THEN
ANDY CAPP
ANECDOTE
ANEMONE
ANGANTYR
ANGEL
ANGELFISH
ANGELICA
ANGELIC LADY
ANGELIKA
ANGELIQUE
ANGELPUSS
ANGELSEY
ANGEL'S HAIR

Gallant boat names which recall past maritime achievements or adventure, are favored and adopted by some modern boaters, and can be easily recognized: ANDREA DORIA, BEAGLE, CALYPSO, FIGARO, FIRECREST, GODSPEED, GYPSY MOTH, ISLANDER, JESTER, KON TIKI, MAYFLOWER, MERRIMAC, MONITOR, NINA, PINTA, POSEIDON, TEDDY, VIKING, TILIKUM, TINKERBELL, TREKKA, SANTA MARIA, SPRAY, TZU HANG, WHISPER, and WANDERER.

AMATUANA
AMAZED
AMAZEMENT
AMAZING GRACE
AMAZON
AMBASSADOR
AMBER
AMBER AIMS
AMBER DEXTROUS
AMBERJACK
AMBER TIDE
AMBIANCE
AMBITIONS
AMBITIOUS
AMBROSIA
AMBUSH
AMBUSHER
AMEN
AMERICA
AMERICANA
AMERICAN BLEND

AMETHYST
AMIDA
AMIGO
AMITIA
AMITY
AMOROUS
AMOS & ANDY
AMO TE
AMOUR
AMPARO
AMPHITRITE
AMPHORA
ANARCHY
ANCHORITE
ANCHOVIE
ANCHOVY
ANCIENT AGE
ANCIENT ECHO
ANDANTE
ANDIAMO
ANDORRAN

ANGIE
ANGIE BABY
_____ ANGLER
ANGLER
ANHINGA
ANIALEA
ANIMAL
ANIMAL HOUSE
ANISETTE
ANKAA
ANKA VON IGLASEE
ANNA LISA
ANNAPOLIS
ANNIE
ANNIE LAURIE
ANNIE O
ANNIE'S ORPHAN
ANNIHILATOR
ANODYNE
ANONYMOUS
ANOTHER DAY

EARLY TRADITION & SUPERSTITIONS

ANOTHER DIMENSION
ANOTHER GIRL
ANOTHER WORLD
ANSEL
ANSER
ANSWER
ANTAGONIST

ANTIGUA
ANTILLES
ANTIQUARIAN
ANTIQUE MYSTIQUE
ANXIETY
ANY 4 FUN
ANY QUESTIONS

APHRODITE'S CHILD
APOGEE
APOLLO
APOLLONIA
APOLLYON
APORIA
APOSTLE

ANTALYA
ANTARES
ANTE
ANTELOPE
ANTE UP
ANTHEA
ANTHEM
ANTICIPATION
ANTIDOTE

ANYTHING GOES
A OVER T
APACHE
APACHE BANDIT
APACHE SUNDANCER
APEX
APHRODISIA
APHRODISIAC
APHRODITE

APOSTLESHIP
APPALACHIAN
APPARITION
APPENDAGE
APPETIZER
APPLAUSE
APPLE BLOSSOM
  WHITE
APPLE JACK

2

Contemporary Conduct:

Modern Guidelines

Selecting your own name can be fun and challenging. The lists provided here surely will help you discover several suitable names from which to choose. Take heart, many, but not all the names listed are in use today. The final choice should be one that feels most comfortable, because once named, that name is unlikely to be changed.

APPLELEAF
APPLE McINTOSH
APPOINTMENT
APPOMATTOX
APRICOT
APRIL FOOL
APRIL LOVE
APROPOS
AQUA LADY
AQUAMARINE
AQUARIAN
AQUARIUS
AQUAVIT
AQUA TECH
AQUATIC DREAM
AQUATIC PROMISE
AQUA _____
AQUILA
AQUITAINE
ARA
ARABELLA
ARAB BARB

ARABELLA
ARABESQUE
ARABIAN NIGHTS
ARAWAK
ARBELLA
ARCA
ARCADES AMBO
ARCADIA
ARCHANGEL
ARCHER
ARCHERFISH
ARCHIE
ARCHRIVAL
ARCTIC ACE
ARCTIC NATICA
ARCTIC TERN
ARCTURUS
ARDENT
ARENA
ARGO
ARGONAUT
ARGOSY

ARGUS
ARGYRONETE
ARIA
ARIADNE
ARIEL
ARIES
ARION
ARISTOCAT
ARISTOCRAT
ARIZONA
ARIZONA _____
ARJUMAND
ARK
ARKADINA
ARKANSAS
ARKANSAS _____
ARMOR ALL
AROUSAL
ARRAM
ARRIVIDERCI
ARROGANT
ARROGANCE

MODERN GUIDELINES

ARROW
ARROWHEAD
ARTEMIS
ARTIFICE O' FORM
ARUNDEL
ASCENSION
ASCENT
ASCOT
ASDUNI
ASGARD
ASHRAM
ASIAN LADY
ASIAN QUEEN
ASPARA
ASPEN
ASPHALT QUEEN
ASPIRANT
ASPIRATION
ASPIRATIONS
ASPIRING
    MILLIONAIRE

ATALANTE
AT EASE
ATLANTA
ATLAS
AT EASE
ATHENA
ATITLAN
ATLANTIC
ATLANTIC _____
ATLANTIC TRADER
ATLANTIS
ATLAS
AT LAST
ATMA
ATOM
ATOMIC
ATRIA
ATRIUM
ATTACHE
ATTRACTION
AUDACIOUS

AUTUMN SONG
AUTUMN SPLENDOR
AUTUMN STAR
AUTUMN WIND
AVALANCHE
AVANT GARDE
AVANTGARDE
AVANT GUARD
AVANTI
AVAS
AVATAR
AVENGER
AVENTINUS
AVENTURA
AVENTURE
AVIARY
AVID
AVIOR
AVOCAT
AVOCET
AVRIL

> *Begin to develop a name for your boat by listing several possiblilities in the space provided on the back pages. Make your final selection from a small list, then "sleep on it" before making your final decision. Consider objectionable features of the name: are there hidden meanings? What about rhyming words? What do the initials spell? What does it spell backwards, i.e., NIAM EZEEUQS.*

ASSAIL
ASSASSIN
ASSERTION
ASSERTIVE
ASSOCIATION
ASSURANCE
ASSURED LADY
ASTARTE
A STEP AHEAD
ASTER
ASTERIA
ASTON
ASTORIA
ASTRAL TRIPPER
ASTRID
ASTRO
ASTRONAUT
ASTRONOMER
ASTRONUT
A SUMMER PLACE
ASYLUM

AUDACITY
AUF GEHTS
AUF WIEDERSEHN
AUK
AUNTIE
AUNTIE MARGE
AUNT JEAN
AUNTY J
AURA
AU REVOIR
AURORA
AUSPICIOUS
AUSSIE
AUSTERE
AUSTRAL
AUSTRALIA
AUTHORITY
AUTHOR'S THEME
AUTUMN
AUTUMN MIST
AUTUMN SHADOWS

AWAKE
AWARD
A W B
AWEIGH
AWESOME
AWOKI
A.W.O.L.
AW SHUKS
AWWWWWWW
AXIOMATIC
AYACHA
AYE AYE
AYE AYE TAINUI
AZENORA
AZTEC
AZTECA
AZULAO
AZURE
AZZURRA

B

BABE
BABES
BABY
BABY BUG
BABY CAKES
BABY DOLL
BABYDOLL
BABYLON
BABY LOVE
BABY MOON
BACARDI
BACARUDA
BACCARAT
BACCHANAL

BAHAMA MAMA
BAHIA MAR
BAIDARKA
BAIT SEEKER
BAJA
BAJA BANDIT
BAKER STREET
BALANDRA
BALBOA
BALD EAGLE
BALEEN
BALENA
BALI
BALI HAI
BALLAD
BALLADEER
BALLET
BALLOU
BALTIMORE
BALZAC
BAMBI
BAMBOO

BARBIE
BARCELONA
BAREFOOT
BARE TRACKS
BARETTA
BARFOOT
BAR GIRL
BAR HARBOUR
BARITONE
BAR MAID
BARNEGAT
BARNEGAT BELLE
BARNICKLES
BARNSWALLOW
BARNWELL
BARON
BARONES
BARONESS
BAROQUE
BAROQUE MUSIC
BARRACUDA
BARRISTER

If you are attracted to a particular name, do some "research" in your unabridged dictionary, or make a short trip to the library to check out any objectionable implications. Since owners rarely change a boat's name, reject those selections which may encourage unpleasant wisecracks.

BACCHANT
BACCHUS
BACH
BACHELOR'S DELIGHT
BACK FIN
BACK OFF
BACK ROOM
BACKBEAT
BACKRUNNER
BACKSTAGE
BADASS
BAD BAD LEROY
   BROWN
BAD BOY
BADGER
BAD HABITS
BAD TO THE BONE
BAER NECESSITY
BAFFLED
BAGATELLE
BAGHEERA
BAHA

BANANA SPLIT
BANDELIAR
BANDERA
BANDERSNATCH
BANDIA JEHANG
BANDIT
BANDOLERO
BANDWAGON
BANGOR PACKET
BANJO
BANKER'S CHOICE
BANKERS TRUST
BANNER DAY
BANSHEE
BANTAN
BANTRY BAY
BARB
BARBADOS
BARBARIAN
BARBEE
BARBERA ANN
BARBERA K.

BARTENDER
BASIC OFFERING
BASIC PLUS
BASQUE
BASSACKWARDS
BASTILLE
BAT
BATFISH
BATMAN
BATTLER
BATTLESHIP
BATTLEWAGON
BAUBLE
BAWDY
BAY BEE
BAY BEE D
BAY BELLE
BAY BIRD
BAY GULL
BAY LEAF
BAYONNE
BAY POINTE

MODERN GUIDELINES

BAY SCOUT
B & B
B-BOP
B.D. JACK
BEACH BUM
BEACH COMBER
BEACHCOMBER
BEAGLE
BEAM'S CHOICE
BEAR
BEAR BOAT
BEAR CAT
BEAR CUB
BEAR DOWN
BEAR FOOTIN'
BEARING UP
BEARN
BEASTIE BETTY
BEATLES
BEATRICE
BEAUFIGHTER
BEAUFISH

BEE FIRST
BEEF TRUST
BEE HIVE
BEEP BEEP
BEE STING
BEESWAX
BEETHOVEN
BEETLE BAILEY
BEFALU
BEFORE
BEGINNING
BEGONIA
BE HERE NOW
BE-IN
BEING COOL
BE IT ALL
BEJEWELED
BE KIND
BEL ESPRIT
BELIEVE 'N MAGIC
BELIVEN
BELLA

BENEVOLENCE
BENGAL
BEN GUNN
BEN TRAVATO
BEOWULF
BEQUEST
BERKSHIRE
BERMUDA
BESIDER
BESSIE LEE
BEST BET
BEST CHANCE
BEST EVER
BEST DEFENSE
BEST FRIENDS
BEST OF TIMES
BEST REGARDS
BEST REVENGE
BEST VIEW
BEST WISHES
BEST YET
BEST _____

Make an effort to avoid selecting a name identical to another boat in your immediate boating area. With the same name you could be blamed for the other fellow's wake, or some other indescretion. Besides, you want to be as unique as possible. Inquiries at local marinas and yacht clubs would be useful to prevent duplication.

BEAUFORT
BEAUJOLAIS
BEAUQUET
BEAUS YEUX
BEAUTIFUL _____
BEAUTIFUL DRUMMER
BEAUTY
BEAUTY'N BEAST
BEAUVIAS
BEAUVIAS NOUVEAU
BEAUX ARTS
BEAVER
BEAVERS DAM
BE BOP
BECHE DE MER
BE DAZZLED
BEDAZZLED
BEDEVILMENT
BEDLAM
BED O' ROSES
BEDOUIN
BEEFEATER

BELLA DONNA
BELLATRIX
BELLA VITA
BELLAROSA
BELLE
BELLE CHATEAU
BELLE ESPRIT
BELLE HARBOUR
BELLE ISLE
BELLE MER
BELLE OF ST MARYS
BELLE POINT
BELLES
BELLINA
BELLSONG
BELLY DANCER
BELOVED
BELT'EM
BELUGA
BELVEDERE
BENGAL TIGER
BENCHMARK

_____ BEST
BETCHA
BETTA MOUSETRAP
BETTER BELIEVE IT
BETTER CHOICE
BETTER MOUSETRAP
BETTER 'N EVER
BETTER LIFE
BETTY BOOP
BETTY GRAY
BETTY GREY
BEVERLEY
BEWITCHED
BEYOND
BIASED LOVE
BIDARKA
BIGAMIST
BIG BAD JOHN
BIG BANANA
BIG BAMBOO
BIG BEAUT
BIG BEEF

BIG BRUTE	BISE	BLAM
BIG BUCKS	BISMARK	BLANK CHECK
BIG BIRD	BIT BY BIT	BLASTER
BIG CASSINO	BIT O' HONEY	BLAZE
BIG DADDY	BITTER END	BLAZER
BIG DEAL	BITTERSWEET	BLAZING STAR
BIG EAGLE	BITTER SWEET	BLAZING _____
BIG FIVE	BIVOUAC	BLEVE
BIG FOOT	BIZET	BLEW BY YOU
BIG MOMA	BLACK ARROW	BLIGH
BIG RED	BLACKBEARD	BLINDED BY THE
BIG SHADOW	BLACKBIRD	LIGHT
BIG STICK	BLACK BIRD	BLINDED BY THE
BIG STORY	BLACK BLAZON	WHITE
BIG SUR	BLACK CAT	BLISS
BIG TIME	BLACKCAT GONE	BLITHE SPIRIT
BIG _____	BLACK COFFEE	BLITHE _____
BIJA	BLACK CORAL	BLITZ
BIKINI	BLACK DUCK	BLOCKBUSTER
BILBAH	BLACK DUTCHESS	BLOODHOUND
BILLBOARD	BLACK FILLY	BLOOD-SWEAT-TEARS

> *Many variations are possible to make your name distinctive from others. Words that sound alike may permit several choices, one of which may suit your interests more than the others: "SEA STAR" can be "C STAR," "SEESTAR," "CEE STAR," "SEASTAR," "SEE STAR," or "C-STAR." A well-chosen name may be retained and taken on to a subsequent boat with the addition of "2," "TWO," "TOO," "TO," "II," "SECOND . . ." (i.e. SECOND CHANCE), or ". . . AGAIN" (i.e. EMPTY POCKETS AGAIN).*

BILLFISH	BLACKFISH	BLOOMERS
BILLY BONES	BLACK FOX	BLOSSOM TIME
BILLY BUD	BLACK GOLD	BLOWN OFFSHORE
BIMINI BLAST	BLACKHAWK	BLOW-UP
_____ BIRD	BLACK ICE	BLUBBER
BINGO	BLACKJACK	BLUE
BINNACLE BABE	BLACK JACK	BLUE ANGLE
BIRD	BLACK MAGIC	BLUE AZMUTH
BIRDARKA	BLACK MARLIN	BLUEBACK
BIRDDOG	BLACK ORCHID	BLUE BANANA
BIRD HOUSE	BLACKPOWDER	BLUE BAYOU
BIRDIE	BLACK SHEEP	BLUEBELL
BIRD OF DAWNING	BLACK SWAN	BLUE BELLE
BIRD O' FREEDOM	BLACK STAR	BLUEBILL
BIRD OF NIGHT	BLACK VELVET	BLUEBIRD
BIRD OF PARADISE	BLACK WATCH	BLUE BIRD
BIRD OF PASSAGE	BLACK WIDOW	BLUEBONNET
BIRD'O PREY	BLACK _____	BLUE CAT
BIRDSONG	BLADE	BLUE CHIP
BIRMINGHAM	BLADER	BLUE CLOUD
BISCUITS	BLADE RUNNER	BLUE CREST

BLUE DEVIL

BLUE DOLPHIN

BLUE DRAGON

BLUE EYES

BLUE FEATHER

BLUE GOOSE

BLUE HEAVEN

BLUE HORIZON

BLUE ICE

BLUEJAY

BLUE JEAN

BLUEFISH

BLUE LADY

BLUE LAW

BLUE LIGHTS

BLUE MAGIC

BLUE MAX

BLUE MIST

BLUE MONDAY

BLUE MOON

BLUE MOON OF
   KENTUCKY

BLUE NEMESIS

BOARD OF _____

BOARD ROOM

BOARDROOM

BOARDWALK

BOASTER

BOAT

BOBBY'S GIRL

BOBCAT

BOB KAT

BOBOLINK

BOBSLED

BOB'S SLED

BOBTAIL

BODACIOUS

BODU DUNI

BODY & SOUL

BODYROOM

BODY WANTS

BOHEMIAN

BOISTEROUS

BOJANGLES

BOLD _____

BOLD ACHIEVEMENT

BON JOUR

BONJOUR TRISTESSE

BONKERS

BONNE AVENTURE

BONNIE

BONNIE LASS

BONNIE LASSIE

BONNIE LOU

BONNIE _____

BONUS BABY

BONUS CHECK

BON VIVANT

BOOBY

BOOGIE FEVER

BOOGIE OOGIE OOGIE

BOODLER

BOOMERANG

BOONDOGGLE

BOOSTER

BOOTLEGGER

BOOTS

BO PEEP

BORDERLINE

Considering how the name will sound "over the air," when others will hear it, could be important, as ship-to-shore radio transmissions may be complicated by a difficult name. Consider the possibility of confusion in a radioed distress signal. Avoid using "MAY DAY," "PAN-PAN," or "SECURITY," as these officially signify important radio announcements.

BLUE NOTE

BLUE RIBBON

BLUE SHADOW

BLUE SHAMROCK

BLUE'S HARP

BLUE SIX

BLUE SKIES

BLUE SKY

BLUE STAR

BLUE SWAN

BLUE TEMPEST

BLUE THUNDER

BLUE WATER

BLUEWATER

BLUE WAVE

BLUE WHALE

BLUE YANKEE

BLUE YONDER

BLUE _____

BLUSHING _____

BLYTHE SPIRIT

BOARD OF TRADE

BOLD ADVENTURE

BOLD ENDEAVOR

BOLD FLIGHT

BOLD PURPOSE

BOLD SPIRIT

BOLD VENTURE

BOLERO

BOLI

BOLL WEEVIL

BOMA CHARGER

BONA FIDE

BONANZA

BONAVENTURA

BONAVENTURE

BON BINI

BON CHANCE

BONDSMAN

BONE

BONE DRY

BONHEUR

BONHOMME RICHARD

BONJOUR

BORED

BORED SUCCESS

BORNE FREE

BORN FREE

BORN TO BE WILD

BORU

BORVA

BOS 'N ARROW

BOSS

BOSS BIRD

BOSS LADY

BOSSY

BOSTON

BOSTON BEAR

BOTTOMLESS

BOTTOM LINE

BOUDOIR

BOUGAINVILLE

BOUNCER

BOUND FOR GLORY

BOUND FOR HEAVEN

BOUND N BLUE

BOUNDER
BOUNDING HOME
BOUNDING MAIN
BOUNDLESS
BOUNTIFUL
BOUNTY
BOUNTY HUNTER
BOUQUET
'BOUT TIME
BOWLEGGED WOMAN
BOW WAVE
BOXER
BOX OFFICE
BOY TOY
BRAHMS
BRANCH OFFICE
BRAND X
BRANDY
BRANDY'S WINE
BRANDYWINE
BRANTA

BREATH OF SPRING
BREEZE
BREEZE AND I
BREWERY WAGON
BREYLL
BRIARPATCH
BRICK BAT
BRIDE OF THE RAIN
BRIEF ENCOUNTER
_____ BRIGADE
BRIGADE
BRIGADOON
BRIGHT DAY
BRIGHT CHILD
BRIGHT FORECAST
BRIGHT FUTURE
BRIGHT HOUR
BRIGHTON BELLE
BRIGHT PROMISE
BRIGHT SIDE
BRIGHT STAR

BROWNIES
BROWN PALACE
BROWN SUGAR
B'RRR
B'RRRRRR
BRUTE
BUBBLE
BUBBLES
BUBBLY
BUCCANEER
BUCKET
BUCKET O' BOLTS
BUCKET OF BOLTS
_____ BUCKET
BUCKEYE
BUCKEYE KID
BUCKPASSER
BUCKS FIZZ
BUCKSHEE
BUCK SHOT
BUCKTIDE

Some repetitive-sounding names, most of which will be recognized, are fully acceptable: BEEP BEEP, BOOGIE OOGIE OOGIE; CAN-CAN, DA DOO RUN RUN; MIRROR MIRROR, NEVER NEVER LAND, NO NO, OUI OUI, POCO POCO, POMPOM, QUACK QUACK, QUICKIE TRICKIE, RIFF RAFF, ROUND AND ROUND, SAY SAY SAY; SHAKE SHAKE SHAKE; SUGAR SUGAR, TA TA, WIG WAG, and WOOF WOOF.

BRASS DRAGON
BRASS MONKEY
BRASS RING
BRASSY
BRASSY BLOND
BRAVADO
BRAVE
BRAVE WORLD
BRAVO
BRAVO PAPA
BRAZEN
BREAK DANCE
BREAKAWAY
BREAK-AWAY
BREAKTHROUGH
BREASTSTROKE
BREATHLESS
BREATHTAKEN
BREATHTAKING
BREATH O' LIFE

BRILLIANCE
BRILLIANT
BRINY
BRINY BENDER
BRISTOL STOMP
BRITANNIA
BRITAN'S CHANCE
BRITE DELIGHT
BRITTANIC
BRITTANY
BROADBILL
BROAD JUMPER
BROADSWORD
BROADWAY
BROCADE
BRONCO
BRONX
BRONZE BOON
BROOKLYN
BROWN

BUCK WELL SPENT
BUDDI
BUDGET BUSTER
BUDGETEER
BUFFALO CHIPS
BUFFOONERY
BUG
BUG DUST
BUGS
BULAA
BULLET
BULLET PROOF
BULLETPROOF
BULLFROG
BULLION
BULL'S EYE
BULL MOOSE
BULRUSH
BUM-BEE
BUMBLE BE

BUMBLE BEE
BUMBLEBEE
BUMBOAT
BUMPER
BUNGALO
BUNKER HILL
BUNNY HOP
BUNSEN BURNER
BUNYIP
BURNING DESIRE
BURNING LOVE
BUSHBABY
BUSHIDO
BUSINESS
BUSTED FLUSH
BUSTER BROWN
BUSY BEE
BUSYBODY
BUSY BODY

C

CABANA
CABARET
CABBAGE PATCH
CABELETTA
CABEWAJA
CABIN
CABOOSE
CABOT
CABRIOLET
CADENCE
CADENZA
CADILLAC

CALLIPYGIAN
CALLIRHOE
CALIBASH
CALIPSO
CALORIC
CALUMET
CALYPSO
CAMARADERIE
CAMBRIA
CAMELLIA
CAMELOT
CAMEO
CAMEO QUEEN
CAMILLA
CAMPECHANO
CANADA
CANADIAN CLUB
CANADIAN MIST
CANADIAN SUNSET

Once the name has been chosen you should select a lettering style suited to your boat's name. There are hundreds of typestyles ranging from traditional to contemporary, block to script, italics, modern, humorous, even computer styles. Most won't suit your needs, but one or more surely will. A professional boat lettering source can be of great help in this, some of which will also provide a complete service of submitting several designs for your selection. Some will suggest colors to be used, and can offer creative graphics including cartoons, logos, or a complete custom design to create a desired effect.

BUTEO
BUTTER AND EGGS
BUTTERCUP
BUTTERFLY
BUTTERED RUM
BUTTERFLY
BUTTERNUT
BUTTINSKY
BUZZED
BWANA
BY DEGREES
BY DESIGN
BYE-BYE
BYE BYE LOVE
BYE YAL
BYGOLLYMIZMOLLY
BY REQUEST
BY STANDER
BY WAYS

CADILLAC COWGIRL
CAGEY
CAHOOTS
CAJUN
CAJUN _____
CAKEWALK
CALAMITY
CALAMAR
CALAMITY JANE
CALCULATED RISK
CALCUTTA
CALEDONIA
CALENDAR GIRL
CALHOUN
CALICO
CALIFORNIA
CALIFORNIA COOLER
CALIFORNIA GIRL
CALIFORNIA _____
CALL GIRL
CALLIOPE

CANADIAN _____
CANBERRA
CAN-CAN
CANCEAUX
CANCER
CANDY
CANDY APPLE
CANDY CANE
CANDY KANE
CANEEL
CAN FI ME
CANIS LUPIS
CANNIBAL
CANNON SHOT
CANNY
CANOPUS
CANOWIE
CAN SEE CLEARLY NOW
CANTANKEROUS
CANTATA

CAN'T STOP
CANVASBACK
CAPABLE
CAPACITOR
CAPELLA
CAPER

CAPRICORNUS
CAPT. HOOK
CAPT. KIRK
CAPTAIN BLIGH
CAPTAIN JACK
CAPTAIN KANGAROO

CARE
CAREER GIRL
CAREFREE
CARE NOT
CARESS
CARE TAKER

CAPE ROUNDER
CAPES
CAP HORN
CAPITAL GAIN
CAPITALISM
CAPRI
CAPRICE
CAPRICIOUS
CAPRICIOUS WOMAN
CAPRICORN

CAPTIVATE
CAPTIVATION
CAPTURED SOUL
CARA
CARAT
CARAVELLE
CARBON COPY
CARDIAC ARREST
CARDINAL
CARDINAL VIRTUE

CARETAKER
CARIAD
CARIB
CARIBBEAN _____
CARIBBEAN LADY
CARIBE
CARILINA LEE
CARILLON
CARINA
CARL GUSTAV

CARMEL
CARMEN
CARMINE CARESS
CARNIVALE
CARNATION
CARNIVAL LADY
CAROLINA
CAROLINA BABY
CAROLINA QUEEN
CAROLINA _____
CAROLINE
CAROUSAL
CAROUSEL
CARPET BAGGER
CARRIC
CARRIE
CARRY ON
CARRIE LYNNE
CARROT
CARROT TOP

CATALIST
CATALYST
CATALYTIC
　CONVERTER
CATANIA
CATAPILLAR
CATAPULT
CATASTROPHIC
CATBIRD
CATCALL
CAT CALL
CATCH 22
CATCLAW
CAT CORNERED
CATENA
CATERPILLAR
CATFISH
CATFISHER
CAT IN THE HAT
CATSASS

CEE _____
CEE CACHE
CEE CALF
CEE CARGOT
CEE CASA
CEE DAWG
CEE DAYS
CEE DREAM
CEE REBEL
CEE SLAVE
CEE TIME
CEE TOY
CEE WATCH
CEE YA
CELEBRATE
CELEBRATION
CELESTE
CELESTIAL ASCENT
CELESTIAL FIXES
CELESTIAL WINDS

Documented yachts are required to have the name and hailing port marked together in some conspicuous place on the hull. Pleasure yachts are not required to have the name on each bow. Commercial vessels must have the name on the port and starboard bows and the hailing port must appear on the stern. The lettering must be at least four inches in size, in a color contrasting with that on the hull, and must be clearly legible and durable.

CARVED STAR
CAR WASH
CASA MIA
CASANOVA
CASCADE
CASH FLOW
CASINO GAL
CASPER
CASTAWAY
CASTAWAYS
CASTILLE
CASTOR
CASUAL
CASUAL LASS
CAT 22
CATACLYSM
CATALACS
CATALAN
CATALIC
CATALINA

CAT'S CRADLE
CAT'S GILL
CATSKILL
CAT'S MEOW
CAT'S PAUSE
CAT'S PAW
CAT WALK
CAT _____
_____ CAT
CAVALE
CAVALIER
CAY LA VEE
CC & WATER
C COMBER
C CONCH
C CRAZY
C CREST
CECILY SKYE
CEDARMAR
CEDAR RUNNER

CELTIC
CELTIC HARP
CENTAURUS
CENTERFOLD
CENTER RING
CENTURION
C.E.O.
CERES
CERRILLOS
C'EST MAGNIFIQUE
C'EST MOI
CHABLIS
CHAIKA
CHAIN GANG
CHAIN REACTOR
CHAIRMAN OF DA
　BOARD
CHALEUR
CHALLENGER
CHAMA

CHAMELEON
CHAMOIS
CHAMOMILE
CHAMPAGNE
CHANCE
CHANCES ARE
CHANCY
CHANNEL FLYER
CHANTEUSE
CHANTILLY
CHANTY
CHAPTER
CHAPTER ELEVEN
CHAPTER TWO
CHAPTER XI
CHARDONNAY
CHARETA
CHARGER
CHARIOTEER
CHARISMA

CHERE AMIE
CHERISH
CHEROKEE
CHERRY BOMB
CHERRYLEAF
CHESAPEAKE
CHESAPEAKE BELLE
CHESAPEAKE HIGH
CHESAPEAKE MISS
CHESAPEAKE _____
CHESHIRE CAT
CHES PIE
CHESSIETER
CHESTNUT
CHEVAL BLANC
CHEYENNE
CHEZ NOUS
CHIANTI
CHICAGO
CHICKADEE

CHITTAGONG
CHIVALROUS
CHIVAS REGAL
CHLOE
CHOCK FULL 'O NUTS
CHOCOLATE CAKE
CHOCOLATE CHIP
CHOCOLATE FUDGE
CHOCOLATE SUNDAE
CHOICE
CHOICE CUT
_____ CHOICE
CHOPPER
CHOREOGRAPHER
CHORUS JIG
CHOSEN ONE
CHRISTI
CHROMED
CHUCK'S STAKE
CHUCK'S STEAK

The size (height and width) of the lettering to be used should be matched to the space available for it, or to the degree of recognition desired. The U.S. Navy may use very small lettering on the largest aircraft carrier, whereas the sponsor of a competition boat surely will want the maximum recognition, perhaps aloft in the sails (if so equipped), on each side of the hull, and across the transom. A large percentage of boats are federally documented, and there are specific regulations concerning the legibility of lettering for these.

CHARLESTON
CHARLIE'S ANGEL
CHARLIE'S CRAB
CHARLOTTE
CHARMER
CHASER
_____ CHASER
CHASTE
CHASTITY
CHATNICLEER
CHATTY
CHAUFFEUR
CHAZMAR
CHE'
CHEAP THRILLS
CHECK MATE
CHECKMATE
CHEERFUL
CHEERLY
CHEERS
CHEQUERS

CHICKEN LITTLE
CHICKEN SHACK
 BOOGIE
CHIEF
CHIEFTAIN
CHILD
CHILD'S PLAY
CHILI PEPPERS
CHIMAERA
CHIMERA
CHIMO
CHINABERRY
CHINA DOLL
CHINCOTEAGUE
CHINOOK
CHINOOKCHIPMUNK
CHIPMONK
CHIP 'N DALE
CHIQUITA
CHIRCANTO
CHIRON

CHUKAR
CHUNKY
CHUTZPAH
CHU-U
CIAO
CICADA
CICATRIX
CID
CIELO
CIMBI
CINCO
CINNABAR
CINSEER LEE
CINTRA
CIRCE
CIRCUMNAVIGATOR
CIRCUMSTANTIAL
 EVIDENCE
CIRCUS
CIRO
CIRRIKEE

MODERN GUIDELINES

CIRRITUS
CIRRUS
CISCO KID
CISCO 'N PANCHO
CISNE BRANCO
CITIUS
CITTADEL
CITY LUCK
CIVILIZED
CLAIR
CLAIR DE LUNE
CLAIRVOYANT
CLAMOUR
CLARENDON
CLARIONET
CLARITY
CLASS ACT
CLASSIC _____
CLASSIC CAT
CLASS OF '_____
CLASSY
CLASSY LADY
CLASSY LASSIE

COBRA
COCHISE
COCKATOO
COCKLESHELL
COCK ROBIN
COCK SURE
COCONUT
CO-CONSPIRATOR
COCOON
COC PIT
C.O.D.
CO ED
COGNAC
COHABITATE
COHOE
COLAS
COLD DUCK
COLD GOLD
COLD SNAP
COLDSTREAMER
COLIN
COLLABORATOR
COLLAGE

COMPANION
COMPASSION
COMPASS ROSE
COMPLETE AT LAST
COMPLETE SILENCE
COMPLEXITY
COMPOSITE
COMPROMISE
COMP TIME
COMPULSION
COM WAT MAY
CON BIRO
CONCEPT
CONCERTO
CONCH
CONCOON
CONCORDE
CONDOR
CONDOR OF BERMUDA
CONFIDANTE
CONFRERE
CONFUCIOUS SAY
CONFUSION

Why, you say, would anyone choose a name like <u>that</u>? Fact is, the most unlikely or unrecognized names listed are real and in use. To understand the choice made by someone, try saying it out loud (like TEHINI or XTASEA). The meaning becomes apparent. Whatever name you choose, you should "feel comfortable" with your choice.

CLEAN ACT
CLEAN AIR
CLEAN WAKE
_____ CLIPPER
CLEAN CONSCIENCE
CLIMAX
CLIPPER DE HARO
CLIPPER ONE
CLOCK OUT
CLOSE ENCOUNTERS
CLOUD 9
CLOUD NINE
CLOUDSONG
CLOUD TEN
CLOUDBURST
CLOUD CHASER
CLOVER
C'MON
COASTER
COAT 'O ARMS
COBALT
COBBERS

COLLECTION
COLLEEN
COLONEL
COLONEL LEE
COLONEL'S LADY
COLONEL'S PRIDE
COLONIAL EXPLORER
COLONIALS
COLORED ONE
COLOR 'O SUNSET
COLOSSUS
COLT
COLUMBINE
COMANCHE
COMANDANTE
COMET
COMMANDANTE
COMMANDO
COMMODORE
COMMON CAUSE
COMMON SENSE
COMMUNION

CONGERE
CONIFER
CONJUROR
CONNAUGHT
CONNECTICUT
CONNEMARA
CONNFUSION
CONNIE
CONNIE D.
CONQUEROR
CONQUEST
CONSENT
CONSERVER
CONSORT
CONSTANCE
CONSTANT
CONSTELLATION
CONSTITUTION
CONSULTANT
CONTAGIOUS
CONTEMPLATION
CONTENDER

CONTENT
CONTENTION
CONTESSA
CONTEST
CONTRAILS
CONTRAIRE
CONTRARY
CONTROLLED CHAOS
CONVERSE
COO
COOKIE
COOKIE CUTTER
_____ COOKIE
COOL _____
COOL BREEZE
COOL CHANGE
COOL FOOL
COOL HAND
CO OP
COOTER
COPESETIC
COP OUT

COSMIC WARRIOR
COSMIC _____
COSMOS
COSTLY SECRET
COTERIE
COTTON CANDY
COUGAR
COUNTACH
COUNTERACT
COUNTERCULTURE
COUNTERPOINT
COUNTESS
COUNTESS MARIA
COUNTESS _____
COUNTLESS HOURS
COUNTRY LADY
COUNTS
COUPLET
COURAGE
COURAGEOUS
COURIER
COURSTORMER

CRAZY _____
_____ CRAZY
CREATIVE DANCER
CREATIVES
CREDIT AGRICOLE
CREEPIN' CHARLIE
CREOLE
CREOLE WOMAN
CRESCENDO
CRESCENT
CREST
CREST DANCER
CRESTED EAGLE
CRESTER
CRESTFLOWER
CRICKET
CRIMAERA
CRIME BUSTER
CRISSCROSS
CRISTOFORO
COLOMBO
CRITICAL MASS

> *More often than not, a chosen name has more than one meaning to the owner, (i.e. SWELL, or WEE LUFF). These meanings may or may not be obvious, as it could refer to something very personal in a way not obvious to the casual observer, perhaps shared only with very close friends, if shared at all: ELSIE MAE, MAY KNOT, JUNE WIL, etc.*

COPS 'N ROBBERS
COQUETTE
COQUINA
CORBEAU
CORDELLA
CORINE
CORKY
CORMORANT
CORNUCOPIA
CORONET
CORPUS DELECTI
CORSAIR
CORVETTE
CORVUS
COSMIC
COSMIC CANOE
COSMIC CLOUDS
COSMIC COWBOY
COSMIC DANCE
COSMIC DUST
COSMIC KID
COSMIC LADY

COURTIN SESHUN
COURT JESTER
COURTSHIP
COVER GIRL
COVE SEEKER
COVIE MARU
COWBOY
COWGIRL
COWPENS
COYOTE
COZY
CRABAPPLE
CRAB CLAWS
CRACKER JACK
CRACKER JACK
CRACKERS
CRACKLIN' ROSIE
CRAZED
CRAZY HORSE
CRAZY LADY
CRAZY LITTLE THING
CRAZY QUESTOR

CRITIC AT LARGE
CRITICS CHOICE
CROATAN
CROISSANT
CROIX DE LORRAINE
CROSSBONES
CROSSBOW
CROSSEA
CROSSFIRE
CROSSROADS
CROSSWINDS
CROW
CROWNED PIPER
CROWNING TOUCH
CROWN JEWELS
CRUISING LADY
CRUNCH
CRUSADER
CRUSOE
CRUZAN
CRUZAN _____
CRUZAN LADY

3

Gadzooks!

Classical, Astrological, Celestial & Philosophical Names

> The names of saints, men and women in the Bible, and the classics, have been used throughout the ages and continue to modern times. These designations may also have a subtle tie-in to the owner: *ADAM'S APPLE, CAMELOT, EVE'S APPLE, GOLIATH, HAMLET, HEROINE, ILIAD, JERICHO, JEZEBEL, MAGI, MONA LISA, PLATO, PROPHET, SANTA ELENA, SANTA MARIA, SANTA PAULA, and SANTA ROSA.*

CRYSTAL
CRYSTAL WAVE
CRYSTAL _____
C SHEL
C.S.S. ALABAMA
C.S.S. REBEL
CUB
CUBIC
CULEBRA
CULER ME GONE
CUPID
CURATIVE POWERS
CURIOSO
CURIOSITY
CURLIE
CURLEW
CURRITUCK
CURTAIN CALL
CUTLASS
CUTTHROAT
CUTTLEFISH

CUTTYHUNK ISLAND
CUTTY SARK
CYANA
CYBELE
CYCLES
CYCLONE
CYGENT
CYGNET
CYGNUS
CYME
CYNA BARR
CYNIC
CYNTHIA
CYNTHIA DAWN

D

D 9
DABBLER
DADDY DID
DADDY DID IT
DADDY DO
DADDY WARBUCKS
DADDY'S
DADDY'S MONEY
DA DOO RON RON
DAD'S DAYDREAM
DAD'S DREAM
DAD'S TOY
DAEDALUS
DAEMON
DAFFODIL
DAGGER
DAGMAR
DAHOLONEGA
DAILY DOUBLE

DAILY DOZE
DAIMOKU
DAINICHITER
DAINTY LADY
DAIQUIRI
DAISY MAE
DAKHALA
DALI
DALLAS
DALLIANCE
DALLS
DAME
DAME D'IROISE
DAMMIT
DAMON & PYTHIAS
DAMSEL
DANA
DANCE CARD
DANCE MUSIC
DANCER
_____ DANCER

DARUMA
DARVON
DARWIN
DAS BOOT
DASH
DASHER
DATURU
DAUMIER
DAUNTLESS
DAUPHIN
DAVY CROCKETT
DAWDLE
DAWNBREAKER
DAWN CHASE
DAWN HORSE
DAWN OF PEACE
DAWN PATROL
DAWN PIPER
DAWN TREADER
DAWN _____
DAY BY DAY

DEBUTANTE
DECADENT
DECENT
DECISION
DECISIVE ONE
DECLARATION OF
    INDEPENDENCE
DECOY
DECRIMINALIZED
DEDICATED
DEE LITE
DEEP DIVER
DEEP PURPLE
DEEPSTAR
DEE VICE
DEFENDER
DEFIANCE
DEFIANT
DEFOE
DEFROSTER
DEISM

Often combined with a personal interest area of the owner, other classical names from literature, art, and philosophy, become highly acceptable boat names: ARABIAN NIGHTS, CAMELOT, CHICKEN LITTLE, DE VINCI, DIFFERENT DRUMMER, HORNBLOWER, IVANHOE, MACBETH, MICHELANGELO, NEMO, OMAR KHAYYAM, OPHELIA, ORIENT EXPRESS, PRIMROSE PATH, ROMEO AND JULIET, SHERLOCK, WALDEN, and WILLIAM TELL.

DANCING QUEEN
DANDELION
DANDY
DANDY GIRL
DANDY ONE
DANDY _____
DANGER ZONE
DAPPER DAN
DARDANELLES
DAREDEVIL
DARIFALU
DARING
DARK HORSE
DARK LADY
DARK MOON
DARK ROAST
DARK STAR
DARLING ONE
DARNIT
DART
DARTER

_____'S DAYDREAM
DAYDREAM
DAY DREAMER
DAYS OFF
DAZED
DAZZLE
DAZZLE ME
DAZZLER
D BASE
DEACON
DEAD HEAD
DEAL 'EM
DEANS LIST
DEARBORN
DEAR JANE
DEBBIE
DEBIT
DEBONAIR
DEBORAH
DEBRA
DE BRIE AUSSI

DEITY
DEJA VIEW
DEJA VU
DEJA VUE
DELAWARE
DELECTABLE
DELFINO
DELI
DELIBERATE
DELICIOUS
DELIGHT
_____ DELIGHT
DELIGHTED
DELILAH
DELIRIUM
DELIRIOUS
DELIVER
DELPHIN
DELPHINA
DELPHINIUM
DELUSIVE

CLASSICAL, ASTROLOGICAL, CELESTIAL & PHILOSOPHICAL

DEMENTED
DEMETER
DEMIJOHN
DEMITASSE
DEMURE
_____ DEN
DENAB
DE NADA
DENALI
DENEBOLA
DENISE
DENNIS THE MENACE
DENSONG

DETOUR
DEUCES WILD
DEUX AMIS
DEVA
DEVASTATOR
DEVILMADEMEDOIT
DEVON DREAM
DEWDROP
DEWY EVE
DEXTEROUS
DHARMA
DHARMA BUM
DIA

DIDACTIC
DIDDLES
DIDDY-WA-DIDDY
DIDO
DIEHARD
DIETY
DIFFERENT DRUMMER
DIG IT
DIJON
DILEMA
DILIGENCE
DILLY
DILLY DALLY

DER BARON
DESCARTES
DESERT FOX
DESHERITE
DESIGN
DESIREE
DESPERADO
DESPOT
DESTINATION
  UNKNOWN
DESTINATION UN NO
DESTINY
DETENTE

DIABOLICAL
DIALECT
DIALOGUE
DIAMANT NOIR
DIAMOND DAYS
DIAMOND HEAD
DIAMOND IN ROUGH
DIAMOND LIL
DIAMONDS
DIANA
DIANE
DIBEK ASUTO
DICHOTOMY

DIMPLES
DIN-A-LEE
DINGO
_____'S DINGHY
DINOSAUR
DIOGENES
DIONYSUS
DIOTE
DIPHDA
DIPSEA
DIRIGO
DIRTY DOZEN
DISARM

DISARMING
DISCIPLE
DISCO DUCK
DISCOVERER
DISCOVERY
DISDAIN
DISINHERITED
DISPATCHER
DISRUPTION
DISTANT DRUM
DISTANT DRUMMER
DISTANT HORIZONS
DISTANT TIME
DISTANT _____
DISTINGUE
DISTRACTION
DISTRAKSHUN
DISTURBANCE
DIS WAY

DOG SOLDIER
DO IT
DOLBY
DOLCE FAR NIENTE
DOLL FIN
DOLL HOUSE
DOLLHOUSE
DOLLY
DOLPHIN
DOMINANT
DOMINIQUE
DOMINO
DON CONEJO
DON JUAN
DONNA
DONNYBROOK
DON QUIXOTE
DON'T LOOK BACK
DON'T PANIC

DOUBLE JEOPARDY
DOUBLE TROUBLE
DOUBLE WHAMMY
DOUBLE _____
DOUBLOON
DOVE
DOVES TALE
DO WAH DIDDY
DOWNHILL RACER
DOWN THE HATCH
DOWN WIND
DOWNWIND HONEY
DOWSEY
DRACO
DRAGGIN ON
DRAGON
_____ DRAGON
DRAGONFLY
DRAGON LADY

Navigational stars, astrological signs of the Zodiac, galaxies and other celestial bodies are frequent sources for inspiration, producing highly pleasing names: ARIES, BLAZING STAR, CAPRICORN, CONSTELLATION, EVENING STAR, GEMINI-JO, HALEY'S COMET (not Halley's), METEOR, ORION, PENSIVE PISCES, POLARIS, POLE STAR, SATURN, SEALESTIAL, SHOOTING STAR, SIDEREAL, SOUTHERN CROSS, STARLIGHT, STELLAR, TAURUS TOM, TROJAN HORSE, TRUSTY STAR, VEGA, and WINTER SOLSTICE.

DITCHDIGGER
DIVA
DIVER
DIVERSION
DIVIDEND
DIVINE GYPSY
DIVINITY
DIXIE
DIXIE LEE
DIXIE _____
DIZZY DAME
D M Z
D N A
DOABLE
DODGE MORGAN
DODGER
DOER
DOGFISH
DOGGIE
_____'S DOGHOUSE

DOODAD
DOODLEBUG
DOODLER
DOODLES
DOONESBURY
DOOZER
DORADE
DORADO
DOROTHEA
DORSAL FIN
DO RUN RUN
DOS AMIGO
DOS CERVEZAS
DOS HERMANOS
D O T
DO THAT TO ME
DOUBLE CROSS
DOUBLECROSS
DOUBLE DARE
DOUBLE EAGLE

DRAGON WINGS
DRAGOON
DRAMBUIE
DREADNOUGHT
DREAM
DREAM BOAT
DREAM BOAT ANNIE
DREAMBOAT
DREAM CHASER
DREAM CUM TRU
DREAM DANCER
DREAMER
DREAMGIRL
_____'S DREAMGIRL
DREAMLIKE
DREAM MACHINE
DREAM MAKER
DREAM ON
DREAMS
DREAMS COME TRU

DREAMS END
DREAMSTATE
DREAM WEAVER
DREAM _____
_____ DREAM
DR. FEEL GOOD
DRIFTER
DRIFT FACTOR
DRIFTWOOD
DRIVEN
DROMEDARY
DROP OUTS
DR DEMENTO
DR SPEED
DR'S ORDERS
DRUM
DRY MARTINI
DUBHE

DUTCH TREAT
DUTCH UNCLE
DUTCH WIND
DUTCHY
DUTIFUL
DUTY FREE
DUVANI
DWARF
DWARFISH
D X
DYLAN
DYNA
DYNAMIC DUO
DYNAMITE
DYNASTY

EASTA EDEN
EAST COAST GIRLS
EASTING DOWN
EASY
EASY DID IT
EASY DOES IT
EASY LIVIN
EASY RIDER
EASY VERTUE
EASY _____
EAT FOAM
EAT MI WAKE
EBBEN FLO
EBULLIENT
EBULLITION
ECCENTRIC
ECHO
ECHOS OF SUMMER

Idealistic or utopian ideas, celestial awareness, and other supreme or heavenly concepts, inspire those who go to sea. These sources of names continue to modern times: ALMOST HEAVEN, ANGEL, BETTER LIFE, DELECTABLE, EUPHORIA, FAIRYLAND, HAPPY HUNTING GROUND, HEAVEN'S GATE, HIGH LIFE, LOFTY, LUSCIOUS, KINGDOM COME, MIRACLE, NATURAL HIGH, PARADISE, (and PAIR-A-DICE), PEARLY GATE, PERFECTION, PIG HEAVEN, PRIME CUT, PROVIDENCE, REDEEMER, SALVATION, SCRUMPTIOUS, SEA TEMPLE, SENSATIONAL, SERENITY, SEVENTH HEAVEN, SHANGRI-LA, SIMPLY PERFECT, THE FORCE, THEOS, THE SOURCE, THEREAFTER, ULTIMATE HIGH, UNSURPASSED, ZEN, ZENITH, and ZEUS.

DUCATS
_____ DUCK
DUCK SOUP
DUCKY
DUDE RANCH
DUDETTE
DUET
DUKE OF WINDSOR
DULCE
DULCINEA
DUMB BROAD
DUN
DUNIT
DUNROWIN
DUSK CHASER
DUSKY DANCE
DUSTY WORK
DUTCHESS

E

EAGER BEAVER
EAGLE
EAGLE CLAN
EAGLE FEATHER
_____ EAGLE
EAGLET
EAREDIL
EARL
EARLY BIRD
EARLY RISER
EARLY TIMES
EASILY
EASILY DONE

ECLAIR
ECLAIREUR
ECLAT
ECLECTIC
ECLIPSE
ECOSYSTEM
ECSTASY
ECSTASY IN MOSHUN
ECSTATIC ADVENTURE
ECUME
ECUREUIL
 D'AQUITAINE
EDDY
EDDY MAKER
_____ EDITION
EDELWEISS
EDITOR IN CHIEF
EDLEWEISS

EDVENTURE
EERE
EFERT LESS
EFFERVESCENT
EGAD
EGO
EGO TRIP
EGO _____
EGRESS
EGRET
E H F
EHO
EHU KAI
EIDER
EIGHT BALL
EILEEN
EIRA
EIRE

ELEUTHERA
ELEVEN
ELEVENTH NIGHT
ELFIN
ELFIN MAGIC
EL GRECO
ELI BANANA
ELIMINATOR
ELINOR
ELITE
ELIXIR
ELLEN
ELLEN JOY
ELLIS BURNS
EL LOBO
ELM
ELMIRA
ELNATH

EMERALD CITY
EMERALD SEAS
EMERALD _____
EMINENT
EMIR
EMMA
EMMANUEL
EMMANUELLE
EMMY
_____ EMOTION
EMPASSANT
EMPATHY
EMPEROR
EMPRESS
_____ EMPRESS
EMPRESS OF BRITIAN
EMPRESS OF CHINA
EMPRESS OF FRANCE

Sparkling, precious, and attractive; "a cut" above the best: ALL THAT GLITTERS, BEDAZZLED, BEJEWELED, BETTER MOUSETRAP, CAMEO, DIAMOND IN ROUGH, DAZZLER, FLASHY, HUMDINGER!, KUGERRAND, LITTLE JEWEL, NONE FINER, NONESUCH, NUGGET, NTH DEGREE, OBJET D'ART, OPAL, PARAGON, PAR EXCELLENCE, PHOENIX, PRIMA, PRISMATIC, PRISSY, PRISTINE, QUICKSILVER, ROMAN CANDLE, SACRED COW, SCINTILLATION, SEA PEARL, SEQUINS, SHIMMERING ANGEL, SIMPATICO, SOOO FINE, SPARKLE, STARDUST, STERLING, STUNNING, SUBLIME, SUCH CLASS, TIFFANY GIRL, TINSEL, TOP BRASS, TOP ECHELON, TOUCHA CLASS, TREASURE, TRULY FAIR, TWENTY-FOUR KARAT, TWICE AS NICE, and VENERABLE.

E K G
ELAINE
ELAN
ELANCER
E LANE
EL BEE
ELDORA
ELDORADO
EL DORADO
ELECTRA
ELECTRIFIED
ELECTRO
ELEGANCE
ELEGANT LADY
ELEGANT MUSIC
ELEGANT _____
ELEKTRA
ELEMENTAL SENSES

ELOISE
ELOPE
ELOQUENT
ELSA
ELSEI
ELSIE MAY
ELTANIN
EL TORO
ELUSION
ELUSIVE
ELVER
ELVERA
ELVIRA
ELVIS
EMANCIPATION
EMBERS
EMERAUDE
EMERALD

EMPRESS SUBARU
EMPRESS _____
EMPRISE
EMPTY POCKETS
EMPTY POCKETS
  AGAIN
EMTEE POKETS
EMU
EN BLOC
ENCHANTE
ENCHANTED
ENCHANTED EVENING
ENCHANTED EYES
ENCHANTED _____
ENCHANTER
ENCHANTING
ENCHANTRESS
ENCLAVE

4

Miss Or Mrs. To The Modern Ms.

The Feminine Influence

Historically, boats have always carried graceful lines and have been cherished and spoken of lovingly by seafaring men: *ANGELIC LADY, DANCING QUEEN, DANDY GIRL, DEMURE, DUTCHESS, EMPRESS, GENTLE LADY, GOLDEN GIRL, HONEY, LADY LOVE, LADY PEARL, MERMAID, MYSTICAL WOMAN, NOBLE LADY, OCEAN QUEEN, QUEEN BESS, REFINED LADY, SEA QUEEN, SENORITA, SOPHISTICATED LADY, SPECIAL MISS, SWEET THING, THE MOST BEAUTIFUL GIRL, UPTOWN GIRL, VIVACIOUS, and WINGED LADY.*

ENCORE
ENCOUNTER
ENDA TIME
ENDANGERED SPECIES
ENDEAVOUR
ENDERI
ENDLESS HASSLE
ENDLESS LOVE
ENDLESS MILE
ENDLESS PROMISE
ENDLESS ROVER
ENDLESS SUMMER
ENDLESS WINDS
ENDLESS _____
ENDO
ENDORPHIN
END RUN
ENDURANCE
ENERGY

ENFANT GATE
ENFORCER
ENGAKU
ENGLISH SPARROW
ENIGMA
ENJOY
ENLIGHTENED
ENOLA GAY
EN PASSANT
EN RAPPORT
EN ROUTE
ENSEMBLE
ENTER COURSE
ENTER LEWD
ENTERPRISE
ENTICER
ENVOLEE
EOAN
EOS

EPATANT
EPEE
EPIC
EPICENTER
EPICURUS
EPILOGUE
EPITOME
EPITOMY
EPOCH
EPR
EPRIS
EQUINOX
EQUITABLE SOLUTION
EREHWON
ERG
ERICA
ERIC HISCOCK
ERIE
ERIE WINDS

THE FEMININE INFLUENCE

ERIK THE RED
ERIN
ERLEE
ERMITAGE
ERN
EROS
EROTIC
EROTICA
ERRANT
ERRONEOUS ZONE
ERSE
ESCAPADE
ESCAPE
ESCARGOT
ESCORT
ESKASONI
ESKIMO _____
ESKIMO EXPRESS

ETHEREAL WINDS
EU
EUCLID
EUGE
EUGENIE
EUPHORIA
EUROCLASS
EURYTHMICS
EVE
EVENING BREEZES
EVENING STAR
_____ EVENT
EVERGLADES
EVER MINE
EVE'S APPLE
EVOLUTION
EXACTA
EXCALIBUR

EXPRESSO
EXPRESS YOURSELF
EXTERMINATOR
EXTRA _____
EXTRACTOR
EXTRAGALACTIC
EXTRANEOUS
EXTRAORDINARY
EXTRAVAGANT
EXTREME
EXTRICATE
EXUBERANT ONE
EYAS
EYE 2 EYE
EYEBRIGHT
EYE CATCHER
EYE CATCH R
EYED 4 LUCK

---

*Lest we forget the more modern femininity: **BLOOMERS, CO ED, COVER GIRL, FEMME FATALE, GLAMOUR GIRL, MISTRESS, NATTY LADY, NAUGHTY GIRL, PASSIONATE MISTRESS, POWDER PUFF, PRETTY BABY, PLAYMATE, QUAINT LI'L LADY, READY MAID, REFINED, RISQUE LADY, ROWDY GIRL, SENSUAL DELIGHT, SEXY THING, SILLY GIRL, SULTRY, SWEETS, TANTALIZER, TEENIE BOPPER, TEMPTRESS, TEN PLUS, TWISTY BRITCHES, WIGGLETTE,** and **WORKING GIRL.***

*MISS, MS, and MRS. labels used in the modern world may join with other words to create a humorous or desired effect: **MISS BEHAVE, MISS CHIEF, MISS DEMEANOR, MISS FIT, MISS FORTUNE, MISS LEAD, MISS REPRESENT, MISS STEAK, MISS TAKE,** and **MS TAKEN.***

ESMERALDA
ESOTERIC ESSENCE
ESPERANZA
ESPRIT
ESPRITE
ESQUELLA
ESSENCE
ESSENE
ESSENTIAL ECSTASY
ESSEX
ESTANCIA
ETCETERA
ETERNAL BLISS
ETERNAL BUM
ETERNAL SEEKER
ETERNAL SUMMER
ETERNAL _____
ETHEREAL

EXCELLENT
EXCHEQUER
EXCITING
EXHILIRATION
EXO
EXODUS
EXOTIC COCKTAIL
EXOTIC DANCER
EXOTIC LAUGHING
EXOTIC MOTION
EXOTIC TAIL
EXOTIC _____
EXPECTATION
EXPECTATIONS
EXPLORER
EXPO
EXPOUND
EXPRESSION

EYE DONE IT
EYE OF THE TIGER
EYEOPENER
EYE OPENER
EYEPIECE
EYES HAVE IT
EYES OPEN
EYRIE
E Z
E Z DAZE
E Z DUS IT
EZEE RIDER
E Z GOER
E Z LIVIN
E Z MONEY
E Z PEACE

F

FA
FAB FOUR
FABULOUS
FABULOUS _____
FACES
FACE VALUE
FACSA LIFE
FACTORY GIRL
FADIGU MAKUNU
FAGIN

FAIRY _____
FAKIR
FALCON
FALLEN ANGEL
FALSTAFF
FAME
FAMILY AFFAIR
FAMILY MATTER
FAMILY WAY
FANATIC
FANCY
FANCY FREE
FANCY _____
FANDANCER
FANDANGO
FANNY HILL
FANSEE
FANTASEA

FASHION PLATE
FAST BREAK
FAST BUCK
FAST COMPANY
FAST ENUFF
FASTER
FASTER ACCESS
FAST FORWARD
FAST LANE
FASTNET
FAST'N LOOSE
FAST PASSAGE
FAST TRACK
FAST _____
FAT CAT
FAT CHANCE
FATE
FATED

Feminine names may also show esteem or shared ownership: BUMBLE BE, BYGOLLYMIZMOLLY, CARILINA LEE, DEE VICE, GINGER FLOWER, JOAN'S ARK, KILLER BE, MOANER LISA, MY CYN, NAN SEA, PARTY PRIS, PATTY CAKE, POLLY'S CRACKER, RAMBLIN' ROSE, RAPSADY, SALLY FORTH, SEALESTIAL, THREE BELLS, WINEE PEG, and WORKER BEE.

Notorious feminine names have inspired salty boat names. One very popular name that accompanies untold thousands of both aircraft and sea craft is MAE WEST. Other sultry names include: DAGMAR, EMMANUELLE, GODIVA, LOLITA, MADAM X, ROSE LEE, SUSIE WONG and XAVIER.

FAI
FAIR BALL
FAIR CHANCE
FAIR DINKUM
FAIR LADY
FAIR SHAKE
FAIRWAY
FAIRWELL
FAIR WIND
FAIR WINDS
FAIR _____
FAIRY
FAIRY GODMOTHER
FAIRYLAND
FAIRY PRINCESS
FAIRY QUEEN
FAIRY TALE
FAIRY TERN

FANTASIA
FANTASY
FANTASY LAND
FANTOM
FARALLON
FARAOUCHE
FARAWAY
FAR CRY
FARE THEE WELL
FAREWELL
FAR FETCHER
FAR FLUNG
FAR HORIZONS
FARMERS DAUGHTER
FAR OUT
FAR SHORES
FAR SIDE
FASCINATION

FATIHU
FATIMA
FAT LADY
FAULTLESS
FAUNA
FAUNUS
FAUST
FAUX PAS
FAVOURITE
FAWN
FAZED
FEARLESS
FEARLESS FOSDICK
FEATHER
FEATHER DUSTER
FEATHER WEIGHT
_____ FEATHER
FEDAYEEN

5

All The World's A Stage:

Arts, Entertainment, Stage, Screen & TV

Stage, screen, TV, and radio can provide the inspiration to find just the "right" name: **AFRICAN QUEEN, AMOS & ANDY, BABY DOLL, BLITHE SPIRIT, CAPTAIN KANGAROO, CAPT. KIRK, CLOSE ENCOUNTERS, COCK ROBIN, DIRTY DOZEN, EASY RIDER, FLINTSTONES, GATOR, GEORGE & GRACIE, GODZILLA, GONE WITH THE WIND, GULLIVER, GUNSMOKE, HARPO, HARRY O., HONEYMOONERS, IMPROMPTU, M*A*S*H, MATINEE, ME JANE, MOONLIGHTING, MUNSTERS, MY ONLY VICE, NEVER SAY NEVER, NO RESPECT, ORKA, PERFORMING ARTS, PICNIC, PILLOW TALK, RAVE REVIEW, SATURDAY NIGHT LIVE, SCOOBY DOO, SESAME STREET, SEVEN YEAR ITCH, SHAMPOO, SKIN FLICK, SMURFS, SOUND OF MUSIC, STAGE FRIGHT, STAGE STRUCK, THE BUTLER DID IT, THE GREAT ESCAPE, THE LONE RANGER, THE SHADOW,** *and* **TOP GUN.**

FEDORA
FEELING BETTER
FEELING FINE
FEELIN GRATE
FEI
FELICIA
FELICITA
FELICITY
FELINE
FELISA
FEMME

FEMME DU CREUX
FEMME FATALE
FENIX
FERDINAND
FEROCIOUS
FERRET
FERVOD
FESTINA TERTIA
FESTIVAL
_____ FESTIVAL
FESTIVALE

FETCH
FETISH
FEVER
FEY
FEZ
F FREDDY
FIANCEE
FIASCO
FIDDLE
FIDDLE DEE
FIDDLER

FIDDLER CRAB
FIDDLER'S GREEN
FIDDLIN ROUND
FIDELITY
FIDUS ACHATES
FIEF
FIERCE
FIERCE PRIDE
FIESTA
FIESTY
FIFTY FIFTY
FIGARO

FINN
FIONA
FIRE ANT
FIREBOX
FIREBRAND
FIRECRACKER
FIRECREST
FIREDRAKE
FIREFIGHTER
FIRE FOX
FIRE THREE
FIREWATER

FIRST TIME EVER
FIRST _____
FISHBONE
FISH FEATHERS
FISHIONABLE
FISHMONGER
FISH'N FOOL
FISHTAIL
FITTEST
FITZ US
FIVE 2 ONE
FIVE BROTHERS

FILET MIGNON
FILLY
FINALE
FINALIST
FINE LINE
FINE LION
FINENESS
FINE ROMANCE
FINESSE
FINE TIME
FINE TUNED
FINISTERRE

FIRING LINE
FIRST BORN
FIRST CLASS
FIRST CHOICE
FIRST DATE
FIRST EDITION
FIRST LADY
FIRST LASS
FIRST MATE
FIRST MILLION
FIRST OUT
FIRST STEP

FIVE ELEMENTS
FIVE STAR
FIZZ ISHUN
FLAIR 4 WIND
FLAMBEAU
FLAMENCO
FLAMER
FLAMINGG
FLAMINGO WARRIOR
FLASHBACK
FLASHDANCE
FLASHDANCER

ARTS, ENTERTAINMENT, STAGE, SCREEN & TV

FLASHER
FLASH GORDON
FLASHLIGHT
FLASH POINT
FLASHY
FLAWLESS
FLEDGING
FLEET
FLEET FEET
FLEETWING
FLESHPOT
FLEUR DE LYS
FLEURY MICHON
FLEXIBLE FLYER
FLEXIBLE LOCATION
FLICKER
FLIER
_____ FLIER

FLOWER POWER
FLOWIN IMAGE
FLUENT
FLUER
FLUNKY
FLUTER
FLY BY
FLY BYE
FLY BY NIGHT
FLYER
FLY CATCHER
FLYCATCHER
FLYING A
FLYING CIRCUS
FLYING CLOUD
FLYING CONCH
FLYING EAST
FLYING ENTERPRISE

FOOLISH PLEASURE
FOOLS GOAL
FOOLS GOLD
FOOTLOOSE
FOOTPRINTS
FORAY
FORCE 8
FOR COMFORT
FOREIGN BORNE
FORERUNNER
FOREVER
FOREVER AND EVER
FORGET HELL
FORIN CEES
FORKED OVER
FORMIDABLE
FOR ONCE IN MY LIFE
FOR PLAY

Well-known comic strips, fables, children's stories, games, playthings, even nursery rhymes, may have multiple meaning to the boat owner:
ALLEY CAT, ALLEY OOP, BATMAN, BAUBLE, BEETLE BAILEY, BETTY BOOP, BINGO, BO PEEP, COCK ROBIN, DENNIS THE MENACE, FAIRY QUEEN, FEARLESS FOSDICK, FOREVER &
EVER, GULLIVER, JACK & JILL, KEYSTONE KOP, KING'S HORSES, LI'L ABNER, MINNIE MOUSE, NEVER NEVER LAND, ONCE UPON A TIME, ORPHAN ANNIE, PAC MAN, PEANUTS, PIGGYBACK, RED WAGON, SNOOPY, SUGAR 'N SPICE, SWEETIE PIE, TEDDY BEAR, THE BRIARPATCH, THE FAR SIDE, TIGHTROPE, TISKET A TASKET, TWEETY BIRD, WOLF!, YO YO, and ZORRO.

FLIGHT
_____ FLIGHT
FLIM FLAM
FLING
FLINTSTONES
FLIPPER
FLIRT
FLIRTATIOUS
FLITZER
FLOPSY
FLORA
FLORENCE
FLORIDA
FLORIDA _____
FLOSSY
FLOTSAM
FLOUNCER
FLOWER

FLYING FISH
FLYIN KESTREL
FLYING SKATE
FLYING _____
FLY SWATTER
FOAM
FOCACCIO
FOE
FOEHN
FOGGY BOTTOM
FOLLOW ME
FOLLY DOLLY
_____ FOLLY
FOMALHAUT
FONDUE
FOOLERY
FOOLISH
FOOLISHNESS

FOR REST
FOR SAIL
FORSAIL
FOR SURE
FORSYTHIA
FORTE
FORTH WORLD
FORT KNOX
FORTUITOUS
FORTUNA
FORTUNATE SON
FORTUNE
FORTUNE COOKIE
FORTUNE HUNTER
FORTUOFUS
FOR XAMPL
FOSTER CHILD
FOUR ACES

FOUR ROSES
FOUR SAIL
FOUR SQUARE ANN
FOUR WINDS
FOXFIRE
FOXHOUND
FOX HUNTER
FOXIE
FOXIE LADY
FOX'N SOX
FOXTROT
FOXY
FOXY LADY
FOXY _____
FRABJOUS
FRAMBOISE
FRANCESCA
FRANGIPANI

FREE FORMS
FREELANCE
FREE SPIRIT
FREE WILL
FREE _____
FREMONT
FRENCH KISS
FRENCH MAID
FRENZY
FREQUENT FLYER
FRESH AIRS
FRESH KID
FRESHSTART
FRESNO
FREYA
FRI
FRIAR
FRIDAY'S CHILD

FUCHSIA
FUDDER MUCKA
FUDDY DUDDY
FUENBARI
FUGITIVE
FUGITIVE WOMAN
FUHIVE
FUJIMO
FULL BLOOM
FULL CIRCLE
FULL DECK
FULL FLUSH
FULL MOON
FULL TILT
FULLY INVOLVED
FUN
FUNBOAT
FUNDAMENTAL

Musical interests and song have influenced many boat owners:
AMADEUS, AMAZING GRACE, BALLADEER, BEATLES,
BEETHOVEN, BLINDED BY THE LIGHT, BLUE MOON,
BRAHMS, ELEGANT MUSIC, FLUTER, HIGH NOTE,
INTERMEZZO, HOT ZIGGETTY, JAZZMAN, JOHANN
STRAUSS, JOY TO THE WORLD, LAST DANCE, LEARNIN'
THE BLUES, LOLLIPOP, LULLABY, LYRICAL LADY,
MAESTRO, MINSTREL, MELODY, MINUET, MOZART, OPERA,
OPUS NO. 1, PAPER MOON, PERFECT CADENCE, QUIET
SONGS, RAG TIME, RHAPSODY, RHUMBA, SCHUBERT, SHINE
ON, SLOW DANCE, SONATA, SOUSA, SYMPHONY, TOE
TAPPER, TOP 40, TUNEFUL, TWOSTEP, and WALTZ.

FRANKIE
FRANNY & ZOEY
FRAPPE
FRAU
FRAULINE
FRECKLES
FRED
FREE AT LAST
FREEBASE
FREEBIRD
FREE & CLEAR
FREE & EASY
FREEBOOTER
FREEDOM
FREEDOM 1
FREE FLIER
FREE FLIGHT
FREE FORM

FRIENDA MINE
FRIENDLY
  PERSUASION
FRIENDSHIP
FRIEND SHIP
FRINGE BENEFIT
FRISBEE
FRISKY
FRITZ DA CAT
FRITZ THE CAT
FROGGIE
FROLIC
FROCKLING BELLE
FROLICIN FROG
FRONTIER SEEKER
FRONTLINE
FROSTED FLAKES
FROU FROU

FUNFORALL
FUNOVIT
FUNKYTOWN
FUNNY BONE
FUNNYBONE
FURIES
FURTLE FANNIE
FURY
FUSION
FUSS BUDGET
FUSSY HUSSY
FUTURIST
FUTURISTIC
FYN
FY SHUN

G

GABBY
GACRUX
GADABOUT
GADFLY
GADGET
GAEA
GAEL
GAIA

GAMECOCK
GAMEPLAN
GAMESTER
GA MIN
GAMUT
GANDER
GANDHI
GANGSTER
GANNYMEDE
GANSTER
GARCON
GARDENIA
GARGANTUAN
GARGOYLE
GARIBALDI
GARNET
GARUDA
GARWOOD
GATE CRASHER

GEB
GEE G
GEE STRING
GEE WHIZ
GEEZER
GEISHA GIRL
GEM
GEMINI
GEMINI-JO
GEM OF _____
GEMSTONE
GEMUTLICH
GENERAL LEE
GENERAL SLOCUM
GENEVIEVE
GENGHIS KHAN
GENIE US
GENIUS
GENTLE BREEZE

Popular music has provided both a nostalgic and a clever source of memorable names: DA DOO RON RON, DO WAH DIDDY, ENDLESS LOVE, EYE OF THE TIGER, FLASHDANCE, GREEN TAMBOURINE, HANG ON SLOOPY, HAPPY TOGETHER, HEY! BABY, HOT DIGGITY, I GOT YOU BABE, JACK'O DIAMONDS, MARYAH, NEW KID IN TOWN, NIGHT SHIFT, PEPPERMINT TWIST, ROCK THE BOAT, SAY YOU SAY ME, ALWAYS, IT'S NOW OR NEVER, SGT. PEPPER, PISTOL PACKING MOMA, SHOO-FLY, SILLY LOVE SONGS, SO FINE, STAYIN' ALIVE, THE LOCO-MOTION, TIME IN A BOTTLE, YELLOW SUBMARINE, and ZIPPITY DOO DAH.

GALA
GALACTIC ODYSSEY
GALACTIC VOYGER
GALACTIC WARRIOR
GALAHAD
GALATEA
GALAVANTER
GALE RIDER
GALILEO
GAL KABIR
GALLANT
GALLEON
GALLIC GIRL
GALVESTON
GAL _____
GALLEGO
GAM
GAMBIT
GAMBOL

GATEWAY
GATHERER
GATOR
GATSBY
GAUCHO
GAUGUIN
GAUGUINS TAHITI
GAUNTLET
GAVE ME SHELTER
GAY 90
GAYE
GAYLARK
GAYNELLE
GAZEBO
GAZELL
GAZELLE
GAZETA
G'DAY
G'DIVER

GENTLE GUIDE
GENTLE LADY
GENTLE _____
GENTRY
GEORGE & GRACIE
GEORGIA CRACKER
GEORGIA MOON
GEORGIAN
GEORGIA PEACH
GEORGIA _____
GEORGIE GIRL
GEPPETTO
GERBAULT
GERTIE
GERTRUDE
GETAWAYS
GETTING THERE
GETTIN' IT
GETTIN' IT ON

6

Nautical Naughtiness

From "Salts" Old & New

Inspired by music, yet carrying multiple meanings, we have:
AFTERNOON DELIGHT, ALL THE WAY, BLEW BY YOU, COOL
CHANGE, DO THAT TO ME, FOR ONCE IN MY LIFE, GREAT
PRETENDER, HEARTBREAK HOTEL, IMPOSSIBLE DREAM,
LEARNIN' THE BLUES, LIGHT MY FIRE, MANY-
SPLENDORED THING, MY DING-A-LING, MY WAY, ORGAN
GRINDER, OVER AND OVER AGAIN, ROCK & ROLL, SAY YOU
SAY ME, SENTIMENTAL JOURNEY, SOMETHIN' STUPID,
TASTE OF HONEY, and TIME AFTER TIME.

Pop music has provided the boat owner with many romantic "good"
girl names: GEORGIE GIRL, ISLAND GIRL, MY GIRL, MY LOVE,
OH, PRETTY WOMAN, OH SHEILA, SHE'S A LADY, THE MOST
BEAUTIFUL GIRL, THREE TIMES A LADY, and YOUNG GIRL.

G GEORGE
GHAXALA
_____ GHOST
GHOSTING
G H Q
GIANT
GIANT STEP
GIATEON
GIBBULA
GIGANTIC
GIGOLO
GILDED EGRET
GIN
GINGERBREAD

GINGER FLOWER
GINGERSNAP
GINGER SNAP
GIN RICKY
GIN RUMIE
GIRI
_____ GIRL
GITANA
GIUSEPPE
GIVE CHASE
GIVEM HELL
GIZMO
GLADIATOR
GLADIOLA

GLADYS
GLAMOUR GIRL
GLASS HARP
GLASS SLIPPER
GLEANER
GLEE
GLEE CLUB
GLENAH
GLIB
GLIDE
GLIDER
GLISEN
GLITZY
GLOBAL NETWORK

FROM "SALTS" OLD & NEW

GLOBAL SCALE
GLOBAL WINDS
GLOBE ROAMER
GLOBE TRAVELLER
GLOBE TROTTER
GLOBE WANDERER
GLOCKENSPIEL
GLOGIRL
GLORIA
GLORIETA
GLORIOUS
GLORIOUS BABY
GLORY
GLORY BE
GLORY BEE
GLORY BOUND
GLOSS ENDEAVOR
_____ GLORY
GLOUCESTER

GOD'S SPEED
GODZILLA
GOES OUT
GOETHE
GO FOR IT
GO GETR
GO GO DANCER
GO GO GIRL
GOING
GOLCONDA
GOLD DIGGER
GOLDEN APPLE OF
    THE SUN
GOLDEN CLOUD
GOLDEN COCKEREL
GOLDEN DAZY
GOLDEN DRAGON
GOLDEN EAGLE
GOLDEN EFFORT

GOLDFISH
GOLD LABEL
GOLD METAL
GOLD RANGER
GOLD RESERVE
GOLD RUSH
GOLD STAR
GOLD _____
GOLEM
GO LIGHTLY
GOLIATH
GOLLIWOG
GOLLY
GONADS
GONE
GONE MAD
GONE WITH THE
    WIND
GONNA BE ALRIGHT

Racy and/or humorous feminists require mentioning: BELLY DANCER, BOWLEGGED WOMAN, CALL GIRL, CENTERFOLD, DIZZY DAME, DUMB BROAD, EXOTIC DANCER, GEISHA GIRL, HOT STUFF, LUSTY LADY, MISS CONDUCT, NAUGHTY GIRL, NAUTILADY, NOBODY'S ANGEL, NYMPHET, SEXY MAMA, SHADY LADY, SIZZLIN SAL, SPRING CHICKEN, STUBBORN MISS, and TOPLESS DANCER. We also know of: HARLOT, SHEWOLF, SUPERTRAMP, THE OTHER BITCH, TRAMP, TROLLOP, VIXEN, and to exclude sexism, HUSTLER, JUST DESSERTS, SEA SLUT, STREAKER, STUCK UP, SURE THING, WHITE TRASH, WILD ONE, and WILD THING.

GLOUCESTER ROCKER
GLO WORM
GLUE POT
GLUTTON
GNAT
GNOMES PLEASER
GNOSTIC
GNU
GO AHEAD
GOBBLER
GOBLIN
GOBLIN'S KISS
GOCART
GODCHILD
GODDESS
_____ GODDESS
GODFATHER
GODIVA
GODSPEED

GOLDEN EYE
GOLDEN FLEECE
GOLDEN FLOWER
GOLDEN GATE
GOLDEN GIRL
GOLDEN GULL
GOLDEN HIND
GOLDEN HOPE
GOLDEN LOTUS
GOLDEN NUGGET
GOLDEN OLDIE
GOLDEN PATH
GOLDEN PELICAN
GOLDEN PHEASANT
GOLDEN SPRAY
GOLDEN SUSAN
GOLDEN SWAN
GOLDEN VOYAGER
GOLDEN _____

GONNA FLY NOW
GONNAGITCHA
GONNA GO
GON WACKI
GONZO
GOOBER
GOOD COMPANY
GOOD COUNSEL
GOOD FRIENDS
GOOD HOPE
GOODIE
GOOD LUCK CHARM
GOOD NEWS
GOOD TIMES
GOOD TIMIN'
GOOD VIBRATIONS
GOOD _____
GO OFF
GOO-KNEE BIRD

GOONEY BIRD
GOOSANDER
GOOSE
GOOSE EGGS

GOT IT MADE
GOT MINE
GOTTA GO
GOTTA WEAR SHADES

_____ GRACE
GRACE DARLING
GRACEFUL TIME
GRACIAS

GOPHER
GORILLA
GOSSAMER
GOTCHA
GOTCHA NOW
GOT IT
GOT IT ALL

GOT THERE
GOT TO BE FREE
GOUGEON
GOURMAND
GOURMET
GO WEST
GRACE

GRACIE FIELDS
GRACKLE
GRADE A
GRADE SCHOOL
GRAF ZEPPELIN
GRAMPS
GRAMPUS

FROM "SALTS" OLD & NEW

GRAN CRU
GRANDAM
GRAND DAME
GRAND FINALE
GRANDIER
GRAND MARNIER
GRANDMERE
GRAND _____
GRAN EMOTION
GRAN-MUDDER
GRANNY
GRANNY NOT
GRAN PLAN
GRAN SLAM
GRAN VIEW
GRAPPIE
GRAPPLER
GRASSHOPPER
GRATIFICIATION
GRAY FOX

GREENFISH
GREEN FLASH
GREEN HIGHLANDER
GREEN LIGHT
GREENPEACE
GREENSBORO
GREEN TAMBOURINE
GREEN THUMB
GREEN WID ENVEE
GREMLIN
GRENADIER
GRENDEL
GRETCHEN
GRETEL
GREY BULL
GREY EAGLE
GREY FOX
GREYFOX
GREYHOUND
GREY SHARK

GUB-GUB
GUESS WHO
GUINEA HEN
GUINEVERE
GUISSEPPE
GUITAR
GULLIVER
GUMBO
GUM DROP
GUNBOAT
GUNGA DIN
GUNG HO
GUNNER
GUNSLINGER
GUNSMOKE
GUPPIE
GUPPY
GURNARD
GURU
GUSTER

Race boaters, fishermen, water skiers, and many other modern, fun-loving folk find much humor in boat names. The "bad" girls of pop music has inspired many of these provocative names: HOT CHILD, LYIN' EYES, MATERIAL GIRL, PARTY GIRL, PARTY DOLL, TEASE, and THE STRIPPER; . . . and to further eliminate sexism, the "bad" boys: BAD BAD LEROY BROWN, BAD TO THE BONE, BIG BAD JOHN, BAD BOY, JUNKYARD DOG, HOUND DOG, and MACK THE KNIFE.

GRAY FILLY
GRAYLING
GRAY MATTA
GRAY MATTER
GREASED LIGHTNING
GREASEPAINT
GREAT BARRIER
  EXPRESS
GREAT BOUNDS
GREAT ESCAPE
GREATEST LOVE
GREAT EXPECTATIONS
GREAT PRETENDER
GREAT WESTERN
GREAT WHITE
GREAT _____
GREBE
GRECIAN QUEEN
GREED
GREENBRIAR

GRIFFIN
GRIMALKIN
GRIM REAPER
GRIPER
GRIS GRIS
GRIZZLY
GROG
GROOVIN'
GROOVY
GROSBEAKE
GROSS!
GROUPER
GROUPIE
GROUSE
GROVEL BEFORE ME
GROWLER
GRRR
G SUIT
GUARDFISH
GUAVA JAM

GUSTO
GUTSY
GWAHIR
GYBE TALK
GYBE TALKIN'GYO
GYPSY
GYPSY MOTH
GYPSY SOLE
GYPSY SOLO
GYPSY SOUL
GYPSY PRINCESS
GYPSY ROVER
GYRATOR
GYRFALCOR

HALFPINT
HALF SPEED
HALF WIT
HALF _____
HALIBUT
HALLEY'S COMET
HALLOO
HALLUCINATION
HALLUCINOGEN
HALO
HALY
HAM
HAMAL
HAMBURG
HAMLET
HAMMERHEAD
HAMRAH
HAMSIN
HANALEI

HAPPY DAZE
HAPPY GO LUCKY
HAPPY HOOKER
HAPPY HOUR
HAPPY HOURS
HAPPY HUNTING
    GROUND
HAPPY OURS
HAPPY TOGETHER
HAPPY _____
HAPUUPUU
HARBINGER
HARBOR LEAVER
HARDBALL
HARD CORE
HARDCORE
HARDER
HARDHEAD
HARD HEAD

H
HABEAS CORPUS
HABITAT
HACKLEBACK
HADER
HAF TO CASE
HAG
HAGAR

Some "bad" characters are very bad, or very "odd": ANTAGONIST, BAD HABITS, BAWDY, BLACK SHEEP, CANTANKEROUS, DESPERADO, DIABOLICAL, FEROCIOUS, HAYWIRE, GONE MAD, INPATIENT, LOCO, MOTLEY, MR. HYDE, NINCOMPOOP, ODDBALL, OUTRAGEOUS, PRANKSTER, PSYCHO KILLER, RACKETEER, RASCAL, RAUCOUS, RELENTLESS, RENEGADE, RUTHLESS, SCALAWAG, SCANDALOUS, SCOUNDREL, STREETGANG, SWINDLER, TORMENTOR, TRICKSTER, TROUBLEMAKER, UNSPARING, VORACIOUS, WEIRDO, WHIPPER SNAPPER, WISECRACKER, and WOMANIZER.

HAGGARD
HA HA HA
HAHA SAN
HAIKU
HAKE
HAKEEM
HALBERD
HALCYON
HALE
HALE IO
HALE KAI
HALEY'S COMET
HALF BREED
HALF FAST
HALF HITCH
HALF MINE
HALF MOON
HALF NOTE
HALF PAID FOR

HANCOCK
HANDEL
HANDMAIDEN
HANDU
HANDY BILLY
HANG 5
HANG FIVE
HANG ON
HANG ON SLOOPY
HANKY PANKY
HAN ME DOWN
HANSEATIC
HANSEL 'N GRETEL
HANUI
HAOLE
HAPI COAT
HAPPI COAT
HAPPINESS
HAPPINESS IS

HARDING
HARD LINE
HARE
HAREBRAINED
HAREM GIRL
HARKNESS
HARLEQUIN
HARLOT
HARMONIC CLOUDS
HARMONY
HARPER VALLEY PTA
HARPO
HARPOON
HARPY
HARRIER
HARRIS
HARRY O.
HARUM SCAREM
HARUM SCARUM

FROM "SALTS" OLD & NEW

HASTY	HEAVENLY TWINS	HETAIROS
HATCHET JACK	HEAVEN SENT	HEY! BABY
HATTIE	HEAVEN'S GATE	HEY HON!
HAUNT	HECTOR	HI BALL
HAUPIA	HEDONISM	HIBISCUS
HAVE MINE	HEDONIST	HIDEAWAY
HAVEN	HEE HAW	_____ HIDEAWAY
HAVOC	HEE HEE	HI FI
HAWG HEAVEN	HEGIRA	HIGH BROW
HAWKBILL	HEIDI	HIGH C
HAWKESBURY	HELD OVER	HIGH CALIBUR
HAWKEYE	HELIOS	HIGH ENERGY
HAWKEYED	HELIUM	HIGHFALUTIN
HAWKSBILL	HELLBENT	HIGH FEVER
_____ HAWK	HELLDIVER	HIGH FLIGHT
HAXED ARGO	HELLION	HIGH HOPES
HAYDN	HELLO GOODBYE	HIGH JINX
HAYWIRE	HENI	HIGHLAND CREAM
HAZARD	HENRIETTE	HIGHLANDER
HEAD BALM	HENRY J. KAISER	HIGH LIFE

Risque and sensual implications are usually socially accepted and are in vogue today: AFTERGLOW, APHRODISIA, BURNING DESIRE, CITY LUCK, COHABITATE, CONTAGIOUS, DALLAS, ENTER COURSE, FOUR PLAY, HOT FLASH, JAILBAIT, LEGAL AGE, LIMERICK, LOVE CHILD, LOVE POTION, MAKE ME, NAUTIBOY, PANTY RAID, PLAY PEN, PURPLE PASSION, RAUNCHY, SEADUCER, SEDUCTION, SEX APPEAL, SHENAN-IGANS, STEPPIN OUT, UNZIP ME, USE ME, and WANT TO.

HEAD HEAVEN	HENRY WAGNER	HIGHLIGHTER
HEADHUNTER	HEPTAGON	HIGH MARK
HEADIN HOME	HER	HIGH NOTE
HEADIN OUT	HERA	HIGH PRIESTESS
HEAD REST	HERALD	HIGH PROFILE
HEADS ABOARD	HERALD OF MORNING	HIGH RISK
HEAD SLED	HERCULEAN	HIGH ROLLER
HEADS UP	HERCULES	HIGH SEA
HEAD WEST	HERE I COME	HIGH SEAS DRIFTER
HEALER	HERE'S TO YA	HIGH TECH
HEART	HERETIC	HIGH TEK
HEARTBREAK HOTEL	HERMAN	HIGH TIDE
HEART OF AMERICA	HERMES	HIGH TIME
HEART OF GOLD	HERMITAGE	HIGH VOLTAGE
HEART OF _____	HERMITS NEST	HIGH WAVE
HEARTH	HEROINE	HIGH _____
HEATHEN	HERON	_____ HIGH
HEATHER	HERRESHOFF	HI HO
HEAT WAVE	HERRING GULL	HI HO SILVER
HEAVEN	HESTRUL	HI JINK

HI JINX
HIJINX
HILITE
HI MAR
HINDMOST
HINI
HIPPIE NO MOE
HIPPO
HIRAM WALKER
HIRONDELLE
HITCHHIKER
HI TECH
HI THERE
HI TIME
HITMAN
HIT MAN
HIVE
HI VELOCITY
HOBBIT
HOBBIT HOLE
HOB GOBLIN

HONEY BABE
HONEY BEE
HONEY BUCKET
HONEY BUNNY
HONEYCHILD
HONEY COMB
HONEY DEW
HONEY DO
HONEYMOON
HONEYMOONERS
HONEY _____
HONKY TONK
HONOR
HOODOO
HOODOO CANOE
HOODWINKED
HOOKAH
HOOKED
HOOKED ON ME
HOOKER TOO
HOOLIGAN

HOT DIGGITY
HOT DOG
HOT ENTREE
HOT FLASH
HOT FLASHES
HOT FOOT
HOT LINE
HOT MUSTARD
HOT PURSUIT
HOT ROD
HOT RUDDERED BUM
HOT SAUCE
HOT SHOT
HOT STUFF
HOT TAMALE
HOT TICKET
HOT TODDY
HOT TUB
HOT ZIGGETTY
HOT _____
HOUDINI

Nautical nautiness is often built into selected names by fun-loving boaters. PURPLE DREAMS, and WET DREAM are occasionally seen, and we know of a PUTTIN OUT. We have mischievous friends who once lived aboard a houseboat named PUSSY GALORE. Although it was undoubtably named for the James Bond character, why was their dinghy named LITTLE BIT?

HOBO
HO CHI ZEN
HOCUS POCUS
HOHOQ
HOKIE HI
HOLD ON TITE
HOGAN
HOG HEAVEN
HOIST
HOLIDAY
HOLLANDIA
HOLSTER
HOLUALOA
HOLY GRAIL
HOMBRE
HOMER
HOMEWORK
HOMING PIGEON
HONEY
HONEY B

HOPE
HOPEFUL ONE
HORACE
HORATIO
    HORNBLOWER
HORIZON
HORIZON SEEKER
HORIZONS
HORNA PLENTY
HORNBLOWER
HORNET
HORN PIPER
HORNPIPER
HORSEFEATHERS
HORSE WITH NO
    NAME
HORUS
HOSTAGE
HOSTEL
HOT CHILD

HOUND
HOUND DOG
HOURI
HOUSTON
HOW FAST
HOWLER
HOW TRI I AM
HOYLE
HU
HUASO
HUBRIS
HUCKLEBERRY
    HOUND
HULA
HULA GIRL
HULUPALA
HUMBOLDT
HUMDINGER!
HUNG
HUNGRY EYE

FROM "SALTS" OLD & NEW

I

HUMMINGBIRD
HUMONGOUS
HUN
HUNKY DORY
HUNTER
HUNTRESS
HURRICANE
HURTS SO GOOD
HUSH
HUSSY
HUSTLE
HUSTLER
HYACINTH
HYDRASLED
HYDRA _____
HYDRO

IANS LASS
IAO
IA ORANA
IBBAK
IBEX
IBID
IBIS
ICARUS
I C B M
ICEBIRD

IDLER
IDLE TIME
IDUN
IDUNIT
IDYLL
IF ONLY
IGLOO
IGNORAMUS
I GOT YOU BABE
IGUANA
IHI
IITOT
IKO
ILAHA
ILE
ILENE

Occasionally, humor is lost on some people, or rather, some things that seem hilarious to some, may not even be funny to others. Tasteful humor is always desirable and usually recognized by boatsmen: ANIMAL HOUSE, ANYTHING GOES, BACHELOR'S DELIGHT, BASSACKWARDS (with last "S" reversed), BROAD JUMPER, CRACKERS, CRAZED, DREAM ON, ERRONEOUS ZONE, FIASCO (with upside down "A"), FLYING A, FUDDER MUCKA, GON WHAKI, GOTTA WEAR SHADES, GRANNY NOT, HALF FAST, HONEY DO, KETCH MEIFYOUCAN, LOOSE CHANGE, MOVING VIOLATION, NECESSARY ROOM, NONSENSE, ORANGE IS UGLY, RHYTHM METHOD, RUNNING BARE, SAILBAD THE SINNER, SUCK EGGS, THORNY DEVIL, TOMATO SLOOP, UP YOURS, WATER CHESTNUT, WHITE GIRL, or WILD GOOSE.

HYDROBOOGIE
HYDRO _____
HYENA
HY LIFE
HY N DRI
HYPERION
HYSSOP

ICEMAN
ICHABOD CRANE
ICHIBAN
ICING
ICY MAY
IDEAL
IDEALIST
IDEAL LADY
IDES
I DID IT
IDIDIT
IDIOSYNCRASY
IDLE
IDLE DICE
IDLE HOURS
IDLE OURS

IL FOGNO
ILIAD
ILLINOIS _____
ILLOGICAL
ILLUMINATE
ILLUMINATED
ILLUMINATION
ILLUSION
ILLUSTRIOUS
IL MORO DI VENEZIA
IL PENSEROSO
IMA FAT KAT
IMAGERY
IMB4U
IMMIGRANT
IMMINENT WIN

7

Lover's Lament:

Romance & Other Emotional Experiences

Throughout history love and love-lost have inspired poets, musicians, writers, romantics, and seamen who have reunited with fine vessels: A'LURE, ADORABLE, BELOVED, BIASED LOVE, BURNING LOVE, CARESS, CHERISH, CRAZY LITTLE THING, DELICIOUS, FIRST TIME EVER, FLIRTATIOUS, GREATEST LOVE, JUST US, LOVE, LOVE AFFAIR, L'AMORE, LOVE SONG, MORNING LOVE, ODE TO LOVE, ONLY LOVE, PERFECT LOVE, PLATONIC LUV, PUPPY LOVE, RAPTURE, ROMANCE, SATISFACTION, SAY YOU SAY ME, TETE A TETE, TIMELESS, TOGETHER, VALENTINE, VERI HAPPY, WE TWO, WILD AFFAIR, YOUNG LOVE, and the more racy: KEEPER, LOVE CHILD, LUSCIOUS, RED HOTS, and SUGARTIME.

IMMORTAL	IMPERATOR	IMPROMPTU
IMP	IMPERIAL SPIRIT	IMPROVISATION
IMPACTER	IMPERSONATE	IMPULSE
IMPALA	IMPETUOUS	IMPULSIVE
IMPATIENS	IMPETUS	IMPULSIVE _____
IMPECCABLE	IMPOSSIBLE DREAM	INA HEARTBEAT

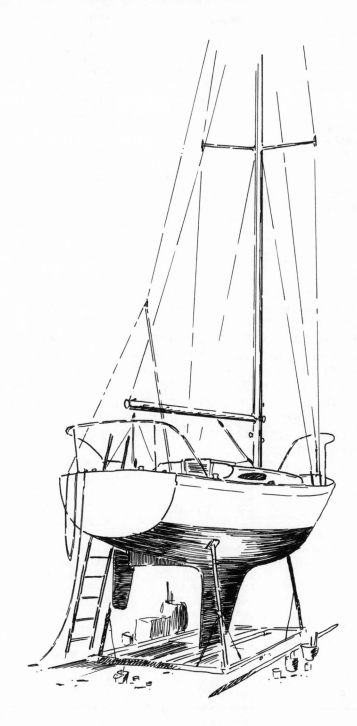

INALIENABLE RIGHT
INAMORTA
INA NUTSHELL
IN A NUTSHELL
INBALANCE
IN BETWEEN
INCA
INCA GOLD
INCARNATE
INCARNATION
INCENSE
INCESSANT
INCOGNITO
IN CONTROL
INCREDIBLE
INCREDIBLE JOURNEY
INCREDIBILY FAMIS
INCUS

INFAMOUS
INFERNO
INFIDEL
INFINITY
INFLAME HER SENSES
INFOQUEST
INFURIATED
ING
INGOT
IN HARMONY
IN HOCK
INISHBOFIN
INITIAL LOVE
IN ITICHINEN
INKA
INKBLOT
INKIE PINKIE
INKY

INSIDER TRADING
INSIGHT
INSIPIT
INSOFAR
INSPIRATION
INSTANT RELIEF
INSTEAD
INSTRUMENT
INSTRUMENTAL
IN STYLE
INTAGLIO
INTANGIBILE
INTEGRITY
INTEND II
INTEND TO GO
INTENSE
INTENSITY
INTENSIVE CARE

An important personal experience or decision may be used for a boat name, and undoubtably will be a topic that draws conversation: **ACQUITTAL, BLOW-UP, CIRCUMSTANTIAL EVIDENCE, CLEAN CONSCIENCE, DOUBLE JEOPARDY, FAMILY WAY, FIRST DATE, FIRST STEP, GOOD COUNSEL, JUNE BRIDE, JUST REWARD, MISTRIAL, MOMENTOUS OCCASION, NEW DIRECTIONS, NEW INITIATIVE, REBELLION, REBOUND, REMEDY, SATISFACTION, SECOND TRY, SHENANIGANS, SHUT OUT, SKINNED, THAT NIGHT, TURNING POINT, VICTIM, WATERLOO, WINDFALL, WON, WONDERSTRUCK,** *and* **WORKIN' IT OUT.**

IN DEBT
INDECENT
INDEED
INDEFATIGABLE
INDELIBLE MARKS
INDEPENDENCE
INDIA INL
INDIANA
INDIANAPOLIS
INDIAN LOVE CALL
INDIAN RIVER
INDIAN SUMMER
INDIGO
INDIGO SEAS
INDOMITABLE
INDUCER
INERTIA
INEZ

IN LAW
INLET RUNNER
IN LIEU
IN LOVE
INMAR
INNATE WANDERER
INNER JOURNEY
INNERMISSION
INNER QUEST
INNIE MARIE
INNISFREE
INN LUV
INNOCENCE
INNOVATION
INPATIENT
INSANITY
INSATIABLE
INSIDER

INTERFACE
INTER GALACTIC
INTERIM
INTERLUDE
INTERMEZZO
INTERMISSION
INTERROGATOR
INTERTWINED
INTIMACY
INTRANSIT
INTREPID
INTRIGUE
INTROVERT
INTRUDER
INTUITION
INTUNE
IN TUNE
INUIT

ROMANCE & OTHER EMOTIONAL EXPERIENCES

INVADER
INVERNESS
INVESTED WELL
INVICTUS
INVINCIBLE
INVISIBLE GYPSY
IN VITA
INWARD JOURNEY
INXS
IO KAI
IOLAIRE
IOLANI
IOLANTHE
IONA
IO NEST
IORQUOIS
IOTA

ISLANDER
ISLAND EXPRESS
ISLAND GIRL
ISLAND PRINCESS
ISLAND QUEEN
ISLAND TRADER
ISLAND _____
_____ ISLAND
ISABEL
ISADORA
ISHMAEL
ISHTAR
ISIS
ISLANDER
ISLAND _____
ISLAND CHASER
ISLAND EXPRESS

ISTAR
IT
ITCHY
ITCHY BITCHY
ITEKI
ITI
IT'S NICE
IT'S NOW OR NEVER
IT'S TIME
ITTSY BITTSY
ITZA-PURLATOO
ITZA SCREAMER
IVAN
IVANHOE
IVE MINE
IVORY TOWER
IXTAPA

Perhaps the owner simply wants to make a statement or challenge to the world: ALIBI, CAKEWALK, CALCULATED RISK, CROSSROADS, DECISION, DISTRACTION, DO IT, EMPATHY, ENDLESS HASSLE, ENSNARLED, EXPRESS YOURSELF, FINE ROMANCE, FIRST OUT, FOOLISHNESS, FOOTLOOSE, FREE SPIRIT, GONE MAD, GOT MINE, GROSS!, HAF TO CASE, HAPPINESS IS, IMPULSE, JUSTIFIED, LACKED TOYS, LIBERATED, LOVE TRIANGLE, NUTS LIKE ME, OUR BABY, PERSNICKETY, PROVE IT, RAN, RAT RACE, REASONS, SCOTFREE, SOLUTION, SPAT, SPECIAL EDITION, STARTIN' OVER, STAYIN' ALIVE, SUMMER FUN, THANKS, THREE GENERATIONS, TOUCHY SUBJECT, UNBOUND, USED, WELL DESERVED, and WISHES.

IPECAC
I Q 150
IRASCIBLE LADY
IRENIC LADY
IRIDESCENT
IRIS
IRISH
IRISH CREAM
IRISH DANCER
IRISH EYES
IRISH MIST
IRISH ROSE
IRISH ROVER
IRISH SMOKE
IRISH _____
IRONY
IRU

ISLAND GAZER
ISLAND GIRL
ISLAND HOPPER
ISLAND LADY
ISLAND QUEEN
ISLAND RUNNER
ISLAND _____
_____ ISLAND
ISLE AU HAUT
ISNOCRIME
ISNT
ISO
ISOLDE
ISOMER
ISOTOPE
ISSA
ISTANBUL

IXTLAN

J

JA
JAADU
JABBERWOCK
JACARANDA
JACK
JACKA DIAMONDS
JACK & JILL

JACK DAW
JACK 'N JILL
JACKNIFE
JACK KNIFE
JACK'O DIAMONDS
JACKPOT
JACK ROBINSON
JACUZZI
JADED
JADED JOURNEY
JAGUAR
JAH
JAHO
JAILBAIT
JALOPY
JAMAICA BAY
JAMBOREE
JAMEN TOAST

JASON'S QUEST
JASPER
JAUNT OFFSHORES
JAVA
JAVELIN
JAY
JAYBIRD
JAZZ
JAZZMAN
JAZZY LADY
JAZZY MOODS
JEAN
JEDI
JELLICE CAT
JELLY BEAN
JEMSTO
JENNIE Q
JENIFER B

JINNI
JINX
JITSU
JIT SURYOKU
JITTERBUG
J JOHNNY
JOANA ARC
JOANNA
JOAN'S ARK
JOCKEYED BOOKS
JOHANN STRAUSS
JOHN DOE
JOHN F. KENNEDY
JOHN FRANCIS
JOHNNY REB
JOHNSON
JOIE
JOIE DE MER

Boat transoms may transmit a departing message to be shared with, or directed at a relationship, or previous time of life: ADIOS, ADIOS AMIGO, ARRIVIDERCI, AU REVOIR, BREAK-AWAY, BYE BYE LOVE, DON'T LOOK BACK, ESCAPADE, GONNA FLY NOW, GOT TO BE FREE, GREAT ESCAPE, GONNAGETCHA, HELLO GOODBYE, IT'S NOW OR NEVER, LAST STRAW, LET'S GO, LIBERTY BELLE, NOGUTSNOGLORY, OUTGOING, RUNAWAY, SAY BYE BYE, SAYONARA, SCOTFREE, SEE YA LATER, SOJOURN, SOLONG, SWANSONG, TEARS HAVE FALLEN, WAY TO GO, WAYWEGO, WENT, WILD ANTICIPATION, and ZATS ALL FOLKS.

JAMES MICHENER
JAMESTOWN
JAMIE LEE
JAMM'D
JAMS
JAM SESSION
JAMTLANDER
JANE
JANE DOE
JANERIC
JANICE
JANNIE
JAN POTT
JANUS
JARGON
JARRE
JASMINE
JASON

JENNIFER
JEOPARDY
JERICHO
JERSEY BOUNCE
JERSEY _____
JESSE JAMES
JESSICA
JESTER
JET
JET SAM
JETSET
JETSTAR
JEWEL
JEZEBEL
JIG SAW
JIM BEAM
JIM DANDY
JIMINY CRICKET

JOIE DE VIVRE
JOKERS WILD
JOLLY GIRLS
JOLLY ROGER
JOLLY RODGER'S
JOLT
JONATHAN
JONNA ARC
JONNA ARK
JONQUIL
JONSON
JORAN
JOSEPHINE
JOSEPH YOUNG
JOSHUA
JOUNCING MAMA
JOURNEY OF LIFE
JOY

8

East Is East & West Is West:

Geographic Origin & Personality Ties

A vessel's attachment to a hailing port or home base may appear in the chosen name, popularized in music: BLUE MOON OF KENTUCKY, CAROLINA QUEEN, MEMPHIS BELLE, PALM BEACH LADY, PRIDE OF BALTIMORE, POOR PEOPLE OF PARIS, SPEEDWELL OF HONG KONG, THE BATTLE OF NEW ORLEANS, T S O P (The Sound of Philadelphia), and YELLOW ROSE OF TEXAS.

JOYCE
JOYOUS ISLE
JOYOUS TIMES
JOY RIDE
JOYS
JOY TO THE WORLD
JOY TOY
J.R.
JUBILANT
JUBILATION
JUBILEE
JUDICIAL PRIVELEGE
JUDO
JUDOIST

JUDY
JUGGERNAUT
JUICE
JU JU BE
JUJITSU
JULI
JULIA
JULIE
JULIET
JULIUS CEDAR
JULY
JUMBIE
JUMBO BUCKS
JUMPING BEAN

JUNEAU
JUNE BRIDE
JUNEBUG
JUNGLE FOWL
JUNGLE QUEEN
JUNGLE WOMAN
JUNGLE _____
JUNIOR
JUNIPER
JUNKET
JUNKYARD DOG
JUNO
JUNSUISEI
JUNTA

JUPITER
JUSTA BOAT
JUSTA GLIMPSE
JUST DESSERTS
JUSTICE PREVAILS
JUSTIFIED
JUSTINIAN
JUSTINE
JUSTIN MORGAN
JUSTINTIME
JUSTIN TIME
JUST REWARD
JUST US
J WALK

KALOOA
KAMA
KAMEHAMEHA
KAMI
KAMIKAZE
KA MOKU O LIMA
KANDO
KANDY KANE
KANE
KANGAROO
KANSAS CITY
KANT BE ME
KANT BE MINE
KAOS
KAPU
KA PUANA
KARAA
KAREN ANN

KAY SEA
KAZOO
KEA
KEALAKEKUA
KEAWE
KEELED ONE
KEEN EDGE
KEEN EDGED FLYER
KEEPER
KEEPIN UP
KEEPSAKE
KEEPS MOVIN
KELLIE
KELPIE
KENDO
KENSPECKLER
KENTUCKY
    GENTLEMAN

Patriotism, national origin, and similiar sentiments can be expressed by dressing out the ship and using proper flag etiquette, by the boat's color scheme and design, and the selection of a name: AMERICA, AMERICAN PATRIOT, AMERICAN PIE, CONSTITUTION, DECLARATION OF INDEPENDENCE, INDEPENDENCE, LIBERTÉ, LIBERTY, LUCKY IRISHMAN, NORSE MAIDEN, PATRIOT, PRIDE 'N SPIRIT, SAUDI PRINCESS, SPANGLED STAR, SPANISH EYES, SPIRIT OF AMERICA, STARS & STRIPES, TAHITI PRINCESS, TURK, VIVE LA LIBERTE, and WANDERING JEW.

K

KAAAWA
KAANAPALI
KABUKI
KACHINA
KADILLAC
KAHALA
KAHUNA
KAILANI
KAIROS
KALA
KALEVALA
KALI
KALIZMA

KAREN LEE
KARMA
KARNES
KA ROSE
KASHAN
KATA
KAT AN MOUSE
KATE
KATHERINE
KATHARINE REBECCA
KATHLYN
KATI SU
KATRINA
KATYDID
KA'U
KAUAI
KAUPOGE
KAVENGA

KEOLOHA
KERMET
KESTREL
KETCH MEIFYACAN
KEVLAR KITTY
KEY OF CEE
KEYNOTE
KEYSTONE KOP
KEY WEST
KHAN
KI
KIALOA
KIAWAH
KICKAPOO
KICKBACKS
KICKS
KID
KID GLOVES

GEOGRAPHIC ORIGIN & PERSONALITY TIES

KID KARMA
KIDDY KAT
KIHEI
KILLDEER
KILLER
KILLER AIN'T
KILLER AUNT
KILLER BE
KILLER BEE
KILLER TOMATO
KILLFISH
KIM
KIMBERLY
KIM CHEE
KIMI
KIMNARAS
KIN
KINDA KOOL

KITE
KIT KAT
KITTEN
KITTIHAWKE
KITTIWAKE
KITTY
KITTYHAWK
KITTY KAT
KIWI
KLEE
KLIMAX EVRETIME
KLONDIKE
KNAVE
KNIFE
KNIGHTHAWK
KNIT WITS
KNOCKERS
KNOCKOUT

KOOKABURRA
KOOKIE MONSTER
KOOL
KOOL BREEZIN
KOOL KAT
KOOL _____
KORKER
KORKIE
KORMAS
KOTO
KOUKLA
KOWLOON
KOW TOW
KRAFTI
KRAKA VIKING
KRAZY KAT
KRIEGIE
KRIOS

Geographical ties provide a useful, interesting and colorful source of memorable boat names: APPOMMATOX, BUCKEYE KID, CALIFORNIA COOLER, CARIBBEAN LADY, CHARDONNAY, GEORGIA PEACH (or MOON, or CRACKER), INDIAN RIVER, IRISH DANCER, KLONDIKE, L.A. EXPRESS, LEXINGTON, MANILA THRILLA, MIAMI NIGHTS, MICHOACAN, MISSISSIPPI QUEEN, NEVADA LADY, OLD NORTH STATE, POTOMAC FEVER, SARATOGA, SEATTLE SUE, SHENANDOAH, SOUTHERN NIGHTS, SOUTHERN SPORTSMAN, SURF CITY, TANGIER, THE CISCO KID, TORTOLA, VENEZIA, WINDEMERE, YANKEE TRADER, and YUKON JACK.

KIND I LIKE
KIND WIND
KINGDOM COME
KINGFISH
KINGFISHER
KING KOLE
KINGS BLUE
KING'S HORSES
KINGSTON
KINSHIP
KINSMAN
KIOLOA
KIOWA
KIP
KISMET
KISSED
_____ KISSES
KISSIN CUZIN

KNOTS ALUCK
KNOTT ME
KNOWER
KNOW HOW
KNUCKLEBONE
KNUCKLE CRACKER
K O
KOA
KOA KANOE
KOAN
KOASTIN
KOCHAB
KODO
KOLE
KONA AU
KONA KOFFEE
KONA WINDS
KON TIKI

KRIS
KRISPY
KRISTINA
KRISTINA MARIE
KRISTINE
KRONOS
KRUGERRAND
KRU KUT
KRUSE'N
KRYPTONITE
KRYPTON
KU
KUDA BOLI
KUDOS
KUDRA
KUE KARD
KUHIO
KULI

KUMQUAT
KUMU
KUNG FU KITTY
KURE
KURT SEA
KURUMBA
KURUN
KUSH TUSH
KUTEY
KYO
KYOKI

L'ADROIT
LADY
LADY A
LADYA MY DREAMS
LADYBIRD
LADY CATHERINE
LADY DU JOUR
LADYFINGER
LADY GREY
LADY ISIS
LADY JANE
LADY LANE
LADY LEX
LADY LIBERTY
LADYLIKE
LADY LILIAN
LADY LOVE
LADYLOVE
LADY LUCK
LADY PEARL
LADY R

L'ALCYON
L'ALLEGRO
LAMASERY
LAMBIE PIE
LAME DUCK
LAMIA
LAMINATED ENTITY
LAMINATION
L'AMORE
LANCELOT
LANCER
LANDED GENTRY
LANDFALL
LANDLUBBERS TOY
LANGLEY
LANI
LANTANA
LANGUID CRUZAN
LA NUIT
LANZE
LAPIS LAZULI

High spirits inspired by school ties, sporting interests, or political sentiments, suggest excellent names and also make a statement for the owner: AGGIE, BLUEBACK, BOOSTER, BOSTON BEAR, C.S.S. REBEL, DIXIE, DIXIE LEE, FORGET HELL, GAMECOCK, HOKIE HI, JOHNNY REB, MUGWUMP, TIGER PAWS, WHISTLING DIXIE, and WOLFPAC.

L

LA BALANCE
LA BELLE
LABILE LASS
LABURNUM
LAC
LA CALMA
LACEWING
LACKED TOYS
LACONIC STEED
LA COUNTESSA
LA CREOLE
LACY LADY
LADA POCH

LADY SLIPPER
LADY WHO WON
LADY _____
_____ LADY
L.A. EXPRESS
L'AFFAIRE DE COEUR
L'AFFAIRE DE MER
LAFFA LOT
LA FLORE
LA FORZA
LAGGARD
L'AGILE
LAGNIAPPE
LA GRANDIERE
LAGUNA
LAGUNE FRAULEIN
LAHAINA
LAIR
LAISSEZ FAIRE
LAKER
LAKOTA

LA PANACE'E
LA POMME
LAPPING WAVES
LAPWING
L'ARDENT
LA RESERVE
LARK
LARKSPUR
LARMOR
LARS PORSENA
L'ARTEMIS DE
   PYTHEAS
LARUS
LAS BRISAS
LASCAR
LASQUETI
L*A*S*S
LASSIE
LAST CALL
LAST CHANCE
LAST COWGIRL

LAST DANCE	L C D	L'EMITAGE
LAST HURRAH	LEADER OF THE PACK	LEMMIE GO
LAST LASS	LEADING EDGE	LEMMING
LAST LADY	LEAF	LEMONADE
LAST STRAW	LEAH	LEMURIA
LAST UNICORN	LEAN CRUISINE	LENA
LAST VENTURE	LEAN MEAN MACHINE	LENITIVE MEDICINE
LAST _____	LEAPFROG	LENORA
LA SURPRISE	LEARNIN' THE BLUES	LEO
LATE BLOOMER	LE BOAT	LEONARDO D V
LATECOMER	LE CHATELINE	LEONARDO DE VINCI
LATIN JAZZ	LECHEROUS LEERS	LEONINE
LATITUDINARIAN	LECHZEN MEER	LEOPARD
LAUGH INN	LE CYGNE	LEOPARD SEAL
LAUGHING BUDDHA	LEDA	LEPRECHAUN
LAUGHING GULL	LEELA	L'ERMITAGE
LAUGHING WATER	LEE RAIL	LE RUSE
LAUNCH PAD	LEEWAY	L'ESCARGOT
LAURA	LEE WORD	LE SEA DUCER
LAUREL	LE FANTASQUE	LES 4 VENTS

Sports fans will be quick to observe that dramatic changes in a name will be made simply by changing from singular to plural: ANGEL(S), ASTRO(S), BENGAL(S), BRAVE(S), BRONCO(S), BROWN(S), CARDINAL(S), CELTIC(S), CHARGER(S), CHIEF(S), COLT(S), COUGAR(S), COWBOY(S), CUB(S), DODGER(S), DOLPHIN(S), EAGLE(S), EXPO(S), GIANT(S), GOPHER(S), HURRICANE(S), JET(S), LAKER(S), MET(S), OILER(S), PACKER(S), PATRIOT(S), RAIDER(S), REDSKIN(S), RAM(S), ROYAL(S), STAR(S), STEELER(S), SULTAN(S), TAR HEEL(S), TIGER(S), VIKING(S), and WILDCAT(S).

LAURIE-ANN	LE FIER	LES MERINGUE
LAUTREC	L'EFFRONTE	LE TERRIBLE
LAVENDER BLU DILLY DILLY	LE FORTUNE	LE TRIOMPHANT
L'AVENTURE	LEFT ALONE	LET'S GO
LA VERANDA	LEFT BRAIN	LEVEL HEADED
LAVERNE	LEGACY	LEVIATHAN
LAWFULLY MINE	LE GAL	LE VIGILANT
LAYLA	LEGAL	LE VIOLETTE
LAY LADY LAY	LEGAL AGE	LEWD FOX
LAZED	LEGAL TENDER	LEXINGTON
LAZ E LAY	LE GAMIN	LIAISON
LAZER	LEGATO	LIBATIONARY LASS
LAZI DAY	LEGISLATER	LIBELLE
LAZY BONES	LEGMAN	LIBERATED
LAZY DAYS	LEHG	LIBERATOR
LAZY DAZE	LEIER	LIBERDADE
LAZY K	LEITER	LIBERTE'
LAZY LIVING	LE LADY	LIBERTINE
LAZY _____	LE MANS	LIBERTY
	LE MISTRAL	LIBERTY AT LAST

9

High Hopes & Swivel Hips

Owner Indentification, Image & Body Parts

Notable personalities and super-achiever images have influenced the
naming of a wide variety of sea craft including military ships: *AHAB,
CAPTAIN BLIGH, CASEY, COLAS, CRISTOFORO COLOMBO,
DALI, DAVY CROCKETT, DODGE MORGAN, GANDHI,
GENERAL LEE, GENGHIS KHAN, HANCOCK, HENRY
WAGNER, HERRESHOFF, JESSE JAMES, JOHN F. KENNEDY,
JONSON, JOSHUA, MARCONI, MAYO, NAPOLEON, NEWTON,
PAUL BUNYON, PAUL REVERE, PONTIAC, RALEIGH, RAMBO,
RICHARD CORY, ROUGH RIDER, SIR THOMAS LIPTON,
TOLSTOY, VAN GOGH, VOLTAIRE, THOREAU, WASHINGTON,*
and *WILLIAM H. AUBRY.*

LIBERTY BELLE	LIDO PLAYER	L I F O
LIBERTY CALL	LIEBCHEN	LIFTED WINDS
LIBIDO	LIEBESTOD	LIFT O WINDS
LIBIDO INTACT	LIEBLING	LIGERO
LIBRA	LIFE IN FAST LANE	LIGHT
LICHTEN DEN ANKER	LIFESAVER	LIGHT FANTASTIC
LICKETY	LIFE STORY	LIGHTFOOT
LICKETY SPLIT	LIFESTREAM	LIGHT MY FIRE
LICORICE STICK	LIFE O' WINDS	LIGHTNING

LIGHTNING BOLT
LIGHTNING BUG
LIGHTNING ROD
LIGHT SHOW
LIGHTS OUT
LIGHTWAVE
LIGHT WORK
LI'L ABNER
LILAC
LILLEDANSKER
LILLIE
LILLY
LILLY PAD
LI'L SMOKER
LI'L SURFER GIRL
LIMELIGHT

LIONHEART
LIPS
LIPSTICK
LIQUID ASSET
LIQUIDITY
LISA
LISBON ANTIGUA
LITEL DO
LITEL DON'T
LITEL DUN
LITE 'N LIVELY
LITHE MODEL
LITHOCRAFT
LITTERATEUR
LITTLE ANNIE
LITTLE BEAR

LITTLE WILLIE
LITTLE WON
LITTLE _____
LIVELY
LIV 'N LUV
LIVELIHOOD
LIVELY LADY
LIVELY VENTURE
LIVERY DOLE
LIVE WINDS
LIVE WIRE
LIZZIE
LIZZIE L
LLAMA
LLADY SIGRID
LOANA

Incorporating proper or "people" names with nautical (or other) terms often creates a completely distinctive and unique name: ALBATROSSI, BAER NECESSITY, BARE BOAT, BLACK JACK, BRANDY'S WINE, CHESHIRE CAT, CHUCK'S STEAK, DENNIS THE MENACE, EFERT LESS, GRAY MATTER, HAREBRAINED, JET SAM, KANDY KANE, KING KOLE, KNOTT ME, KURT SEA, LEE RAIL, MICK LIGHT, OLIVER'S TWIST, PERRY'S WINKLE, QUICK LEE, RAIN BO, RAY FISH, RAZOR SHARPE, RICK O'SHAY, ROMIN' KNOWS, ROWEBOAT, SAUER DOUGH, SCOTTFREE, SMART ALEC, TAYLOR MADE, TEDDY BARE, TOM BOY, TOMMYHAWK, TWIN BILL, TWO MORROW, UPPER HAN, VAN TASTIC, VERY LEE, VIC TORY, WATER WOOLF, WET WILLIE, WHIP POOR WILL, WILD HARE, WILL POWER, WILLY WISPE, WINDOW PANE, WITT'S END, WRIGHT WAYS, and WYNSONG.

LIMERICK
LIMIKA
LIMPET
L'IMPETUEUSE
LIMU
L'INCOMPRISE
LINDA CAROL
LINDO
L'INDOSCRETE
LING
LINGERIE
LINGIN
LINGO
LINGERIE
L'INSOLENT
LIONESS
LIONFISH

LITTLE BIRD
LITTLE BIT
LITTLE BOOZER
LITTLE CHUM
LITTLE DARLIN'
LITTLE DIPPER
LITTLE DITTY
LITTLE FEAT
LITTLE JEANNIE
LITTLE JEWEL
LITTLE LADY
LITTLE ROCK
LITTLE SISTER
LITTLE SUSIE
LITTLE TOOT
LITTLE UPROAR
LITTLE WALTER

LOBO
LOBSTER
LOCAREC
LOCH
LOCH NESS
LOCO
LOCO MOTIVE
LOCOWEED
LOCURA
LODE STAR
LODESTAR
LODESTONE
LOFTY
LOFTY LADY
LOG CANOE
LOGGERHEAD
LOGICAL CHOICE

OWNER IDENTIFICATION, IMAGE & BODY PARTS

LOGO
LOITERER
LOLA
LOLITA
LOLLIPOP
LOLLYGAG
LONDON DRY
LONDON LIGHT
LONG DISTANCE
LONE AT LAST
LONE BULL
LONE EAGLE
LONE ELK
LONER
LONE RANGER
LONE WANDERER
LONE WOLF
LONE _____
LONG COOL WOMAN
LONG SHOT
LONE STAR

LORIAN
LORRAINE
LOST ARK
LOTSA BUCKS
LOTSA LOOT
LOTSA LUCK
LOTSA TIME
LOTSA WIND
LOTTIE
LOTUS
LOTUS LEAF
LOU
LOUCHURA
LOUISVILLE
LOVE
LOVE AFFAIR
LOVEBIRD
LOVE CHILD
LOVE IT
LOVE LETTERS
LOVELY DAYS

LUCKY LASS
LUCKY MOPPIE
LUCKY SHOT
LUCKY STRIKE
LUCKY _____
_____ LUCKY
LUCY
LUDWIG II
LUFTCHEN
LULLABY
LULL A BYE
LU LU
LULU
LUMAHAI
LUMINARY ABOARD
LUMINOUS LASS
LUNA
LUNAR LADY
LUNATIC
LUNATIC FRINGE
LUPINE

A few letters, taken from various family names, may be combined in various ways to make your boat name unique. Make innovations as they please you. Marie and Tommy could become MAR-TOM, MARTOM, or TOMMY M, for example. Betsy, Jean and Carolyn could become BETJACAN, BET JA CAN, U BET JA CAN, or even UBETJACAN. Or the name or last-name initial may combined nautically:
THE SEVEN C's.

LONGBOW
LONG GONE
LONG RYDER
LONGSHOT
LONO
LOOKFAR
LOOKING GLASS
LOOKS FAST
LOOKS LIKE WE MADE
    IT
LOON
LOONEY TUNES
LOON'S NEST
LOOSE CHANGE
LOOT
LOR
LORBI
LORDA LIGHT
LORELEI
LORELIE
LORFINDU

LOVE ME TENDER
LOVEN MONEY
LOVE POTION
LOVERING
LOVERS
LOVE SONG
LOVE TRIANGLE
LOVE _____
_____ LOVE
LOW BID
LOWRY
LOYAL CONVERT
LOYALTY
LUCE
LUCIBELLE
LUCID
LUCKED OUT
LUCKY
LUCKY CHANCE
LUCKY CHOICE
LUCKY IRISHMAN

LUSCIOUS
LUSCIOUS LADY
LUSCIOUS RECIPE
LUSITANIA
LUST
LUST 4 LIFE
LUSTFUL
LUSTY
LUSTY DUSTY
LUSTY LADY
LUV 'N LIFE
LUVSAVER
LUZON
LYDIA
LYIN' EYES
LYING LADY
LYNNE
LYNX
LYRA
LYRICAL LADY
LYRICAL LASSY

LYRICIST
LYRIC ODE
LYRIC WINDS
LYRISCH
L.Y. SPEAR

M

MAALUD
MABEL
MABELLENE

MACK THE KNIFE
MACROCOSM
MACTRIM
MADAM
MADAMS
MADAM X
MADCAP
MADEIRA
MADE ME
MADEMOISELLE
MADE OUT
MADGE
MAD HADDER
MADHATTER

MAGIC CARPET RIDE
MAGIC DRAGON
MAGIC FOR SAIL
MAGIC HEMPEL
MAGIC MOMENT
MAGIC MORN
MAGIC MUSHROOM
MAGIC O' SAILING
MAGIC POTION
MAGIC WORKER
MAGIC _____
_____ MAGIC
MAGISTER
MAGNANIMOUS

MACAQUE
MACAROON
MACAW
MACBETH
MA CHERE
MACHETE
MACHINE GUN
MA CHERRIE
MACH ONE
MACHTS NICHTS
MACKEREL

MADNESS INC.
MADONNA
MAESTRO
MAE WEST
MAGDALENE
MAGENTA LADY
MAGGIE
MAGI
MAGIC
MAGICAL
MAGICAL MACHINE

MAGNIFICA
MAGNIFICANT
MAGNIFICANT
  OBSESSION
MAGNIFICENT
MAGNIFICO
MAGNIFIQUE
MAGNOLIA
MAGNOLIA BLOSSOM
MAGNUM
MAGNUM OPUS

OWNER IDENTIFICATION, IMAGE & BODY PARTS

MAGPIE
MAHALO
MAHARANI
MAHARISHI
MAHATMA
MAHI MAHI
MAH JONG
MAHOGANY RUSH
MAHOUT
MAHO ZUKAI
MAID
MAIDEN HAIR
MAID OF EARLEY
MAID OF HONOR
_____ MAID
MAINE
MAIN FLOW
MAINLINE

MAKING WAVES
MAKO
MALAGUENA
MALAMUTE
MAL DE MER
MALGRE'TOUT
MALIBU
MALIGAWA
MALIHINI
MALTED MILK
M & M
MAMA
MAMA'S BOY
MAMA'S MINK
MAMA'S PEARL
MAMA'S _____
MAMBO
MAMIE

MANTRA
MANU IWA
MANU KAI
MANUKAI
MANX CAT
MANY-SPLENDORED
   THING
MANZANITA
MAPLE
MAP MAKER
MARATHON
MARATHON MARINER
MARAUDER
MARBLEHEAD
MARCELLA
MARCH HARE
MARCY
MARDI GRAS

A boat name may reflect the owner's personality or self-perception. It may be a nickname or "handle," invented by others similar to Citizen's Band (CB) radio call names: BIG BAMBOO, BIG MAMA, BOOTLEGGER, BRASSY BLOND, COLORED ONE, COMIC, COWGIRL, CUT UP, FOX HUNTER, GOODIE, HARDHEAD, HIGH FALUTIN', HUCKLEBERRY HOUND, JESTER, MAVERICK, MOTHER DUCK, RAMBLIN' ROSE, ROAD RUNNER, SIZZLIN' SAL, SMILIN' MAN, SMOOTH OPERATOR, SPACY, STORYTELLER, SWASHBUCKLER, SUGAR DADDY, SUPERSTAR, THE CANDYMAN, TROUBLE MAKER, WHEELER DEALER, WICKED WANDA, and WILD OATS.

MAINSPRING
MAINSTAY
MAI TAI
MAITENES
MAITRE
MAJEB
MAJESTIC
MAJESTIC LADY
MAJIC
MAJOR DOMO
MAJOR FORCE
MAJOR MOTION
MAKAI
MAKE A DETOUR
MAKE MY DAY
MAKENA
MAKING DO
MAKIN' IT

MANANA
MANATEE
MANDALA
MANDATE
MANDOLIN
MANDRAKE
MANDY
MANET
MANGO
MANHATTAN
MANIA
MANICORE
MANILA THRILLA
MANNA
MANNERS
MAN O' WAR
MANTA
MANTICORE

MARESIA
MARGARITA
MARGUERITE
MARIA
MARIACHI
MARIAH
MARIANNE
MARIE
MARIELLA
MARIETTE
MARIGOLD
MARIKA
MARINA FLEER
MARINER
MARINER'S BLISS
MARIONETTE
MARKAB
MARKIN' TIME

MARKSMAN
MARK TWAIN
MARLONETTE
MARMALADE
MARMALADE SKIES
MARQUES
MARQUESA
MARQUETRY
MARRY ME
MARSHMELLOW
MARTEN
MARTHA
MARTINI
MARTINIQUE
MARVEL
MARY

MAS TARDES
MASTERMIND
MASTERPIECE
MASTER PLAN
MASTERSTROKE
MASTIFF
MAST MASTER
MATADOR
MATERIAL GIRL
MATERIAL WORLD
MATCHLESS
MATHIN MOSHUN
MATINEE
MATOU
MATRIX
MAUKA MAMA

M.C. ESCHER
McCOY
MEADOW LADY
MEANDER
MEANDERER
MECCA
MEDICINE HAT
MEDICINE MAN
MEDICINE WOMAN
MEDITATION
MEDIUMSHIP
MEEK 'N MERRY
MEGAN B.
MEIN LIEBCHEN
ME JANE
MELL O

Other desirable names suggest nobility and refined qualities:
COMPASSION, COURAGEOUS, CHIVALROUS, DAUNTLESS, ENDURANCE, FAULTLESS, FEARLESS, FLAWLESS, HONOURABLE, IMPECCABLE, INDOMITABLE, INTEGRITY, PATIENCE, PRUDENCE, RELIABLE, RIGHT STUFF, TENACIOUS, UNBENDING, UNDAUNTED, VALIANT, VANITY, VENERABLE, WELL BEHAVED, and ZEALOUS.

Unblemished character traits and aspirations produce highly memorable and polished boat names: **ADMIRABLE, CHARISMA, CHARMER, CRUSADER, ENDEAVOUR, ENTERPRISE, FINESSE, HARMONY, HONOR, INDEPENDENCE, MAGNANIMOUS, MOXIE, PURITAN, PURITY, SCRUPLES, SIMPLICITY, TO WIN, TRANQUILITY, UPLIFTER, VANITY, and VIGILANCE.**

MARYAH
MARY JANE
MARYLAND
MARY LOU
MAS
MAS ALLA
MASCARA NOMORE
MASCOT
M*A*S*H
MASINGH
MASSA
MASSACHUSETTS
MASSEUSE
MASSINGLY
MASQUERADE
MAST ABEAM

MAUI WOWIE
MAUREEN
MAVERICK
MAVIS
MAX
MAX FUN
MAXIMA
MAXINE
MAVERICK
MAY
MAYA
MAYBELLENE
MAYFLOWER
MAYFLY
MAY KNOT
MAYO

MELLO LADY
MELLOW MAMA
MELLO YELLO
MELO
MELODY
MELODY MAKER
MEMO
MEMORABLE
MEMORIAM
MEMORY
MEMPHIS
MEMPHIS BELLE
MENAGE A TROIS
MENDED HEART
MENEHUNE
MENKAR

OWNER IDENTIFICATION, IMAGE & BODY PARTS

MENKENT
MEQUERO
MERCEDES GULLWING
_____'S MERCEDES
MERCI
MERCURIAL
MERCURY
MERENGUE
MERICA
MERIDIAN
MERIDIEN
MERLIN
MERMAID
MEROPE
MERRIMAC
MERRY GALES
MERRYMAKER
MERRYMAN

MICHELLE
MICHELANGELO
MICHI
MICHOACAN
MICKEY MOUSE
MICK LITE
MID AGE CRISIS
MIDNIGHT PASSAGE
MIDNIGHT PASSION
MIDNIGHT PROSE
MIDNIGHT RIDER
MIDNIGHT SUN
MIDTOWN
MIDWINTER'S DREAM
MIGRAINE
MIGRANT
MIGRATOR
MIGRATORY

MINERVA
MINGLER
MINI MITE
MINK
MINNEY
MINNIE MOUSE
MINOU
MINSTREL
MINTAKA
MINTED MEADE
MINT JULIP
MINUET
MINX
MIRACLE
MIRAGE
MIRIAM
MIRO
MIRROR

Playfully wicked modern boat owners have designated their boats:
**AUDACITY, BAFFLED, BOASTER, BOOBY, BUFFOONERY,
CONFUSION, CONTAGIOUS, DILEMMA, DRIVEN, ENIGMA,
HARUM SCARUM, HAVOC, HEDONIST, HUSTLER,
IGNORAMUS, IMPETUOUS, INSANITY, LUNATIC, MADNESS,
MISCHIEF, INCOMPOOP, NONSENSE, OBSESSION,
OUTRAGEOUS, PANDEMONIUM, PANIC, PERPLEXED,
RAGAMUFFIN, RAGE, RAW TALENT, RENEGADE, REVENGE,
RUFFIAN, SCAPEGPOAT, SCREW LOOSE, SHOW OFF,
SMARTIE PANTS, TANTRUM, TRAMP, TRUANT, VANDAL,
WAYWARD SON, WOMANIZER, and YELLOW FEVER.**

MERRYMENT
MERRY ROVER
MERRYTHOUGHT
MESCALARO
MESDAMES
MESMERIZING
MESSENGER
MESSIN' ABOUT
MET
METAPHOR
METAPHYSICAL
METEOR
MEUNIERE
MEXICAN HATDANCE
MHAIRI DHONN
MIAMI NIGHTS
MIAMI VICE
MIAPLACIDUS

MIGRATORY BIRD
MIKO
MILDRED'S MERCEDES
MILENE
MILES DAVIS
MILIEU
MILLE FLUERS
MILROSE
MIME
MIMI
MIMIC
MI MIS TAKE
MIMOSA
MINDFUL
MIND SET
MINDSWEEPER
MIND TOOL
MINE

MIRROR MIRROR
MIRTH
MIRTHFUL
MIRTHFUL
   MESSENGER
MISCHEVIOUS
MISCHIEF
MISHA
MISS
MISS BEHAVE
MISS B HAVIN
MISS BUDWEISER
MISS CHIEF
MISS CONDUCT
MISS D
MISS DANGEROUS
MISS DEMEANOR
MISS DON Q. RUM

MISS FIT	M'LOVE	MONKEY BUSINESS
MISS FORTUNE	M'LUV	MONKEY ISLAND
MISS I. SSIPPI	MMMMMMM	MONKFISH
MISSISSIPPI	Mmmmmmmmmmmm	MONSOON
MISSISSIPPI GAMBLER	M MOTHER	MONSTER
MISSISSIPPI QUEEN	MOANER LISA	MONTANA
MISSISSIPPI _____	MOBJACK	MONTPELIER
MILL LEAD	MOCCASIN	MOODS
MISS MO	MOCKINGBIRD	MOODY BLUES
MISSOURI	MODERN MATURITY	MOON BEAM
MISSOURI _____	MODISH	MOONBEAM
MISS REPRESENT	MODUS OPERANDI	MOON BOW
MISS-RICH-KAT	MOHAWK	MOONCHILD
MISS STEAK	MOHICAN	MOONDANCER
MISS T	MOIA	MOONDAWN
MISS TAKE	MOJAVE	MOON DRAGON
MISS TAKEN	MOJO	MOON GAZER
MISS TERRY	MOLLY	MOONGLOW

Since some boats can be fairly expensive, the cost, or source of funds may be humorously expressed, or alluded to, in the names: AFFLUENT, ALIMONY, BEEF TRUST, BEQUEST, BIG BUCKS, BLANK CHECK, BONUS CHECK, CAPITAL GAIN, CASH FLOW, FIRST MILLION, INVESTED WELL, JOCKEYED BOOKS, KICKBACKS, LIQUIDITY, LOOSE CHANGE, LOTSA BUCKS, LOW BID, MAMA'S MINK, ONLEE MUNEE, OLD MONEY, OVERTIME, PAID FOR, PAY OFF, PENNY PINCHER, PRICE I PAID, PROMOTION, RAISE 'N PAY, RATE INCREASE, REAL DEAL, REAL ESTATE, SERIOUS MONEY, SHE'S MINE, SOFT SELL, TRUST FUND, WINDFALL, WINNING BID, and YOUTHFUL TYCOON.

MISS TRESS	MOMENTOUS	MOONISH
MISSUS	OCCASION	MOONLIGHT
MISSY	MOMENTS	MOONLIGHT
MISS _____	MOMI	GAMBLER
_____ MISS	MOMMY	MOONLIGHTING
MISTER CLEAN	MONA	MOON LIGHT RIDE
MISTIQUE	MONAD	MOONLIGHT RIDE
MISTRAL	MONA LISA	MOONLIGHT SONATA
MISTRESS	MON AMI	MOON PIE
MISTRIAL	MONAMI	MOONRAKER
MISTY	MONARCH	MOONSEEKER
MISTY _____	MONASTERY	MOONSET
MISTY BLUE	MONDAYS FLOWERS	MOON SHADOW
MISTY MORN	MONDO	MOONSHADOW
MISTY RAY	MONGOOSE	MOONSHINE
MITHRA	MONIQUE	MOONSHINER
MI TOY	MONITOR	MOONSTONE
MIZZLE TOFF	MONKEY BIZNEZZ	MOONTALK

OWNER IDENTIFICATION, IMAGE & BODY PARTS

MOONTIGER
MOON _____
MOORISH IDOL
MOPPIE
MORE APPARITIONS
MORE FOOLISHNESS
MORGENMUFFEL
MORNING BELLS
MORNING CLOUD
MORNING GLORY
MORNING LIGHT
MORNING LOVE
MORNING MIST
MORNING PASSAGE
MORNING STAR
MORNINGTIDE
MORNINGTOWN
MORNING _____

MOTHER WATERS
MOTION
_____ MOTION
MOTIVE UNKNOWN
MOTLEY
MOULIN A VENT
MOUSEKATEER
MOVING VIOLATION
MOVIN' ON
MOVIN' STAR
MOXIE
MOZART
MR. BANJO
MR. BILL
MR. BOSTON
MR. CHIPS
MR. E. US
MR. GOODBAR

MUSKETEER
MUSSEL
MUSTANG
MUSTER
MY BABY
MY COMPANION
MY CYN
MY DING-A-LING
MY ETCHINGS
MY EVERYTHING
MY GAIL
MY GAL
MY GIRL
MY HAPPINESS
MY HAREM
MY IDEA
MY KID
MY LIFE

We have also noted with hilarity, several high-dollar boats dubbed: CHAPTER ELEVEN, CLEAR PROFIT, DADDY'S MONEY, INHOC, LADY WHO WON, MY WIFE WORKS, NARY A CENT, ONLY CHILD, PO BOY, POOR HOUSE, PRICE OF EGGS, SHOESTRING, SPOILED ROTTEN, STUD FEES, SUCH LUCK, TALK'S CHEAP, THANKS DAD, TIGHTWAD, TOUGH TIMES, VAGRANT, and WELFARE.

A devil-may-care attitude may be also expressed: BORN TO BE WILD, COME WAT MAY, SANS SOUCI, SERENDIPITY, TAKE ME, WHENEVER, WHO CARES, WILD ABANDON, and WILD 'N FREE.

_____ MORNING
MORPHEUS
MORPHINE
MORROW ALWAYS
   COMES
MORTAGED DREAM
MOSEY
MO SHUN
MOSIKA ALMA
MOSQUITO
MOSSBUNKER
MOSTLY MAGIC
MOSTLY MINE
MOTA
MOTAVITION
MOTHER DUCK
MOTHER EARTH
MOTHERSHIP

MR. HYDE
MR. _____
MS. _____
MS. EASY
MS. STAKE
MU
MUD IN YOUR EYE
MUG-RAFFIN
MUGWUMP
MUIR
MULTI TRAUMA
MUMURS
MUNSTERS
MURAL
MURDLE
MUSE
MUSK
MUSKATEER

MY LOVE
MY MERCEDES
MY MS. STAKE
MYNA
MYOKO
MYONLY VICE
MY PAULINE
MYRAID WATERS
MYSONGS
MY STEADY
MYSTERIOUS
MYSTERY
MYSTERY LADY
MYSTERY'S CHILD
MYSTIC
MYSTICAL WOMAN
MYSTICAL WORKER
MYSTIC BABE

MYSTIC LAWS
MYSTIC MORN
MYTHIC IMAGE
MYTH MAKER
MYTH OF MALHAM
MY TURN
MY WAY
MY WIFE'S MINK
MY WIFE WORKS
MY YACHT
MY _____

NADA MAS
NADINE
NAGEL
NAGLFAR
NAHEMA
NAIAD
NAIADS
NAIF
NAIM
NAIVETE
NALDA
NAMASTA
NAMASTE
NAMELESS
NAMESAKE
NAMU
NANA

NARRAGANSET
NARRATOR
NARWHAL
NARY A CENT
NASCENCE
NASHA
NASHALLAH
NASHANI
NASHIRA
NASIBU
NASSAU
NASTURTIUM
NASTY LADY
NATALISA
NATASHA
NATIVE CHASER
NATIVE DANCER

The human anatomy, or its capabilities, a dear subject, has prompted some unexpectedly original boat names: ALL HEART, AT EASE, BIG FOOT, BITTER END, BLUE EYES, BODY & SOUL, BREATH O' LIFE, CHUNKY, DIMPLES, EYES OPEN, FACES, FLEET FEET, FUNNY BONE, GIANT STEP, GREEN THUMB, HALF FAST, FRECKLES, HARD HEAD, HAWKEYE, HEART, HUNG, HUNGRY EYE, ITCHY, KNOCKERS, KUSH TUSH, KNUCKLEBONE, LIPS, MENDED HEART, OUTWARD LEG, PEG LEG, PERFECT TOUCH, POONTANG, PRIVATE EYES, SMILES, SPREAD EAGLE, TAKES BALLS, TALLYWHACKER, TEENY-WEENIE, TINEY HINEY, TOOTH 'N NAIL, TRACHEA, UMBILICAL, WHISKERS, WHITE KNUCKLES, WHOPPER, WIGGLE, WILD TUSH, WISHBONE, WATERCOCK, WILDEYED and YELLOWFINGER.

N

NAALEHU
NAASHI
NABEMA
NABILA
NABOB
NACHBETEN
NACHBIS
NACHSOMMER
NACRE

NANAI
NANCY
NANI
NANI KAI
NANNA
NANNY
NAN SEA
NANTAHALA
NANTUCKET
NAOMI
NA PALI
NAPLES
NAPOLEON
NAP TIME
NARCISSUS
NARCOTIZED
NARD

NATIVE GIRL
NATIVE SON
NATIVE VAHINE
NATIVE _____
NATURAL HIGH
NATURALIST
NATURALLY FINE
NATURE ATR BEST
NAUGHTY GIRL
NAUGHTY NICKY
NAURU
NAUTI BABY
NAUTIBOY
NAUTI COW
NAUTICAL LADY
NAUTICAL WEAVER
NAUTICAL

10

Life, Livelihood, And Liquor

Owner's Profession, Vessel's Use, Trade Names

> The vessel's intended use, or activity, may suggest a fitting and
> descriptive name: *ADVENTURER, ANGLER, COPS 'N ROBBERS,*
> *DEEP DIVER, DISCOVERY, DRAGNET, FIREFIGHTER,*
> *G'DIVER, GETAWAY, GREENPEACE, INLET RUNNER, OCEAN*
> *SALVOR, TRANSPLANTER, PILOT, PURSUER, RECOVERY,*
> *SALVAGER, SEAGOER, SEALANDER, TENDER, THRASHER,*
> *TROPICAL TRADER, SEA SCOUT, VOYAGER, WATERBEARER,*
> *and WATERMAN.*

NAUTICAL _____	NEBEL	NEEDS FULFILLED
NAUTIGAL	NEBULA	NEE NEE
NAUTILADY	NEBULOUS	NEFARIOUS
NAUTILUS	NEBULOUS DAZE	NEFERTITI
NAUTI_____	NECESSARY EVIL	NEGLIGE
NAVAJO	NECESSARY ROOM	NEHEMIAH
NAVALONG	NECKING AT SEA	NEHRU
NAVIGABLE PALACE	NECTAR	NEIMAN
NAVAGABLE PLANET	NECTARINE	NELSIE
NAVIGATION BOUND	NECTAR O' GODS	NEMESIS
NAVY BRAT	NE DAY	NEMESIS 4 U
NEAP TIDE	NEEDLE	NEMO

NEOCLASSIC
NEON GAL
NEOPHYTE
NEPENTHE
NEPENTHIAN
NEPTUNE

NERVE CENTER
NERVELESS
NERVY
NESBIT
NESSIE
NESSUS

NEVADA KID
NEVADA LADY
NEVADA _____
NEVER NEGLECTED
NEVER NEVER LAND
NEVER NORMAL

NEPTUNE'S DOLLY
NEPTUNE'S EXPRESS
NEPTUNE'S FOLLY
NEREID
NERENDA
NEREUS
NERO

NEST
NEST EGG
NESTLING
NESTOR
NETHERWORLD
NEUTRON
NEVADA

NEVER QUIT
NEVER SAY NEVER
NEVER SURRENDER
NEVER _____
NEVIS
NEW AGE
NEW & IMPROVED

NEW AN IMPROVED	NIAM EZEEUQS	NINE BELLES
NEW APPROACH	NIBBLED ME	NIP'N TUCK
NEW BEDFORD	NICE'N NAUTY	NIPPON
NEW DEAL	NICE VICE	NIRVANA
NEW DIRECTIONS	NICHTRAUCHER	NISEI
NEW DREAMS	NICHT WHAR	NITISSIMA
NEWFANGLED	NICKERCHEN	NIT PIC
NEWFANGLED TOY	NICKERING FILLY	NIXE
NEW HAMPSHIRE	NICOLE	NIXIE
NEW HORIZON	NIECE NANCY	NJORTH
NEW HORIZONS	NIETZSCHE	NO.2 SESAME'S TREAT
NEWICK	NIFTY	NO APOLOGY
NEW INITIATIVE	NIGHTCAP	NOB HILL
NEW JERSEY	NIGHT CRAWLER	NOBLE LADY
NEW KID IN TOWN	NIGHT CROSSING	NOBLEMAN
NEW LIFE	NIGHT FLYER	NOBLE ONE
NEW MEXICO	NIGHT HAWK	NOBLESSE OBLIGE
NEW MOON	NIGHTINGALE	NOBLE WARRIOR
NEW ORLEANS	NIGHTLY NEWS	NOBODY'S ANGEL
NEWPORT	NIGHT MARE	NOBODY'S FOOL

Perhaps the name will allude to the boat as a refuge to share, or an enticement to attract others: HIDEAWAY, LA REFUGE, MY ETCHINGS, OASIS, QUARTERS, RAVISH YOU, REACHIN' INN, RELIEF, ROOM WITH A VIEW, ROVER COME OVER, SANCTUM, SEA ABODE, SEX MACHINE, STRONGHOLD, SUGARSHACK, SUITOR, TAKE ME, TENDER TRAP, TURN ON, TWO CAN, and UNWED.

NEW SCENARIOS	NIGHT MEETINGS	NO BOUNDS
NEWSENCE	NIGHT MOVES	NO BREAKS
NEWSWORTHY	NIGHT 'N GAIL	NOBUL
NEWSY	NIGHT OWL	NOBULL
NEWT	NIGHT RANGER	NO BULL
NEWTON	NIGHT RIDER	NO CALORIES
NEW TRAILS	NIGHT SHIFT	NOCTURNAL BIRD
NEW WAVE	NIGHT SILENCE	NOCTURNE
NEW WIFE	NIGHT SPARKLER	NODDY
NEW WIFE'S TOY	NIGHT TIGER	NO DEBTS
NEW YORK	NIGHT TRAIN	NO DOUBT
NEW YORK NEW YORK	NIGHT _____	NO EXCUSES
NEW _____	NIKE	NO FENCES
NEX DOOR NAYBOR	NIKRIMI	NO FRILLS
NEXT NEW WORLD	NILE	NOGUTSNOGLORY
NEXT WAVE	NIMBLE	NOH
NEXUS	NIMBLE FOX	NO HANGERS ON
NEZ PERCE	NIMBUS	NO JUSTICE
NIAGRA	NIMROD	NO LESS
NIAN	NINA	NO LESS ON MORE

NO LIE
NOMAD
NO MAME
NO MAME BOAT
NOM DE GUERRE
NO MERCI
NO MERCY
NONCOM
NONE FINER
NONESUCH
NON FAT
NON HERO
NO NICHE FITS
NO NO
NON-PROFIT
NONSENSE
NON SEQUITOR
NONSTOP
NO STRINGS

NORTHERN ROVER
NORTHWEST PASSAGE
NORTHWIND
NORTH WIND
NORWIND
NO SO
NO STOPPING
NO STRINGERS
NOT 4 EVERY 1
NOTABLE
NOTHER LADY
NOTHINGLESS
NOTIONS
NOTION TO GO
NOT JUS US
NOT QUITE
NOT-SO
NOTTINGHAM
NOT TO WORRY

NUBILE LASS
NUBILE PROFILE
NUEVO
NUGGET
NUIT
NUNKI
NUT CRACKER
NUTCRACKER
NUTHATCH
NUTMEG
NUTS LIKE ME
NUZZLING NYMPH
NYEEMA
NYMPH
NYMPHE
NYMPHET
NYMPHO
N Y S E

Oftentimes the owner's profession (or other's) suggests an appropriate name: ASTRONUT, AUTHOR'S THEME, BUDGETEER, CARPET BAGGER, COLONEL'S LADY, CONSULTANT, CRIME BUSTER, ENFORCER, EXTRACTOR, EYES HAVE IT, FREELANCE, HITMAN, IN LAW, JAZZMAN, KNIT WITS, LE GAL, LITHOCRAFT, NOVELIST, OVERDRAFT, PRIME INTEREST, PARADOX, POETESS, R & D, ROUGHNECK, RUG RAT, SANDMAN, SATIRIST, SAW BONES, SCHOOL MARM, SCRIBBLER, SLEUTH, SLUMLORD, TRIAL TACTICS, TROOPER, TROUBLE SHOOTER, VEN DOOR, and WEEKEND WARRIOR.

NONSUCH
NOONTIDE
NOON TIDE
NO QUESTION
NORA
NORDIC BEAUTY
NORD WIND
NO RESPECT
NORMANDIE
NORMAN MACLEAN
NORSE MAIDEN
NORTH CAROLINA
NORTHER
NORTHERN DANCER
NORTHERN LIGHT
NORTHERN LIGHTS
NORTHERN MAID
NORTHERN PRINCESS
NORTHERN RANGER

NOUGAT
NOUVEAU RICHE
NOUVELLE
NOUVELLE DANSE
NOVA
NOVA ESPERO
NOVANET
NOVELIST
NOVICE
NOW
NO WHITHER
NOW VOYGER
NOXEMA
N T H °
NTH DEGREE
NU
NUANCE
NUBBIN
NUBILE DANCER

O

O
OAHU
OASIS
OBA CHAMA
OBAD
OBAGUS
OBDURATE
OBEDIENT

OWNER'S PROFESSION, VESSEL'S USE, TRADE NAMES

OBEDIENT WIFE
OBE WAN KNOBE
OBI
OBITER DICTUM
OBJECTIVE PURITY
OBJECT LESSON
OBJECT TROUVE
OBJET D'ART
OBLIGATO
OBLIGE ME
OBLIVION
OBSERVATORY
OBSESSED
OBSESSION
_____ OBSESSION
OBSIDIAN
OCARINA

OCEAN PRINCE
OCEAN PRINCESS
OCEAN QUEEN
OCEAN RETRIEVER
OCEAN REWARD
OCEAN ROAMER
OCEAN SALVOR
OCEAN SUNLIGHT
OCEAN TRAMP
OCEANUS
OCEAN WINDS
OCEAN _____
OCELOT
OCHRE
OCTAVE
OCTET
OCTOBER WIND

OEDIPUS
OEUVRE
OFFBEAT
OFF CAMPUS
OFF HOUR
OFFLINE
OFF MI ROK R
OFF 'N RUNNING
OFFSHORE CRUZER
OFFSHORE LADY
OFFSPRING
OFFTIME
OFFWEGO
OGI
OGLE ME
OGLETHORPE
OGRE

Interesting and humorous names are employed for a desired effect. Imagine the doctor's office telling someone the doctor is in INTENSIVE CARE; or a secretary saying the boss has gone to the BACK ROOM, BRANCH OFFICE, BOARDROOM, or is on APPOINTMENT, OCCUPATIONAL THERAPY, OVERTIME, STRICTLY BIZZ, or WORK STATION. He (or she) even may be: A.W.O.L., OUT OF REACH, having NIGHT MEETINGS, on LIGHT WORK, OCCASIONALLY OUT, OFF HOUR, ON TIME, on COMP TIME, or working on PAGE ONE, R & R, STOCKS 'N BONDS, or on WALL STREET. He (or she) could even be working on RETIREMENT, PRIORITIES, or caught in RUSH HOUR. Many of these names are actually in use.

OCCASIONALLY OUT
OCCLUSIONS
OCCULT LADY
OCCUPATIONAL
  THERAPY
OCEAN CHARGER
OCEAN EAGLE
OCEAN EDDY
OCEANFAST
OCEANIA
OCEANIC
OCEAN KING
OCEAN LASSIE
OCEAN NYMPH
OCEAN ODYSSEY
OCEAN ORBIT
OCEAN PIPER

OCTOPUSSY
OCULAR
ODALISK
ODD A SEA
ODDBALL
ODDITY
ODDS'N ENDS
ODDS MAKER
O DEED
ODE
ODE II
ODE TO
ODE TO BILLY JOE
ODE TO JOY
ODE OT LOVE
ODIN
ODYSSEY

OH
OH ACES
OHARA
OH BABY
OH GIRL
OHIO
OHIO _____
OHKA
OH MY
OHO
OH OH
OH, PRETTY WOMAN
OH SHEILA
OH YEAH
OIKOS
OIL EMBARGO
OILER

OISEAU DE FEU
OJAI
OJIBWA
OJO
O.J.T.
O K
O'KEEFE

OLD FASHIONED
OLD FITZGERALD
OLD FORESTER
OLD GRANDAD
OLD IRONSIDES
OLD JINTS
OLD MONEY

OLD _____
OLE
OLEANDER
OLEMA
OLE MAID
OLE TIMER
OLIO

OKEYDOKE
OKLAHOMA
OKLAHOMA!
OKLAHOMA _____
OKRA
OLD BLUE
OLD CHARTER
OLD CROW

OLD MR BOSTON
OLD 'N BOLD
OLD NORSE
OLD NORTH STATE
OLD OVERHOLT
OLD SALT
OLD SMUGGLER
OLD TAYLOR

OLIVA
OLIVE
OLIVE BRANCH
OLIVER'S TWIST
OLIVINE
OLOMPALI
OLYMPIA
OLYMPIC

OWNER'S PROFESSION, VESSEL'S USE, TRADE NAMES

OM
OMAHA
OMAR
OMAR KHAYYAM
OMEGA
OMEN
OMERTA
OMNI
OMNISCIENCE
OMOO
OM SHANTI
ONANCE
ON AND ON
ON A PEDESTAL
ON CAMPUS
ONCE UPON A TIME
ONDINE
ONE ACE
ONE ALONE
ONE DAY AT A TIME

ONONDAGA
ON 'N ON
ONSHITSU
ONSLAUGHT
ONSLOW
ONTARIO
ON TIME
ONYX
OO
OODLES
OOGLE
OOH-OUI
OOMPAPA
OONAH
OOO-LA-LA
Ooooh
OOO WEE
Ooo-Weeee
OOPS
OOPSY DAISEY

OPULENT OPTION
OPUS
OPUS 1
OPUS 19
OPUS 29
OPUS NO. 1
O QUEEN
ORACLE
ORANGE BLOSSOM
ORANGE IS UGLY
ORB
ORBITER
ORCA
ORCHID
ORCHID SEEKER
ORENDA
OREO
ORFF
ORGAN GRINDER
ORIANA

Trade or brand names may be appropriate either for commercial reasons, some personal tie-in or humorous connection to the owner, or function of the boat: AIRBUS, APPLE MCINTOSH, BIT O' HONEY, BLUE RIBBON, BOJANGLES, CHOCK FULL O' NUTS, HEAVENLY TWINS, LUCKY STRIKE, M & M, MARY JANE, MISS BUDWEISER, MISTER CLEAN, PAYDAY, MODERN MATURITY, MR. GOODBAR, PORSCHE TURBO, POWERHOUSE, SNICKERS, SOVRAN, TRUE TEMPER, WESTERN SIZZLER, and XEROX COPY.

ONE EYED JACK
ONE FIFTH
ONEIDA
O'NEILL
ONELINE
ONELINER
ONE-LINER
ONE SUITE
ONE TRUE LOVE
ONE _____
_____ ONE
ON GOING
ONION PATCH
ONKAHYA
ONLEE MUNEE
ONLINE
ONLY CHILD
ONLY LOVE
ONLY LUST
ONO

O ORANGE
OPAKAPAKA
OPAL
OPAL EYE
OP ART
OPERA
OPHELIA
OPIATED
O.P.M.
OPOSSUM
OPPORTUNE
OPS
OPSIMATHY
OPTI GAL
OPTIGAL
OPTIMA
OPTIMAL
OPTIMUM
OPTION PLAY
OPULENCE

ORIENTAL LADY
ORIENT EXPRESS
ORIENT XPRESS
ORIENT _____
ORIGAMI
ORIGINAL SIN
ORIOLE
ORION
ORKA
OR KNOT
ORNERY
ORNOMEL
ORPHAN
ORPHAN ANNIE
ORRIS
ORSO DEL MARE
ORTI
ORTOLAN
ORYGIN
OSAGE

OSAKA
OSIER
OSIO
OSPRAY
OSPREY
OSPREY CHASER
OSPREY'S SHADOW
OSTLER
OSTRICH
OSWEGO T
O.T.
OTHER WOMAN
OTTAWA
OTTER
OUI
OUI OUI
OUIJA BOARD
OUR BAY BEE
OUR DREAM

OUTLAW SLOOP
OUTLOOK
OUT OF REACH
OUT OF TOUCH
OUT ON A WHIM
OUTRAGE
OUTRAGED
OUTRAGEOUS
OUTRE
OUTRIDER
OUTSIDER
OUTSTANDER
OUT T'PASTURE
OUTWARD LEG
OUZO
OVER & OVER AGAIN
OVERDRAFT
OVER EASY
OVERJOYED

P

PAANGA
PACEMAKER
PACER
PACHECO
PACIFER
PACIFIST
PAC JAN
PACKAGE DEAL
PACE SETTER
PACER

We have known quite a few boats with liquor names, possibly combined with either the owner's name, or sentiments, or some other subtle connection: ANCIENT AGE, BEAM'S CHOICE, BEEFEATER, CANADIAN CLUB, COLD DUCK, CREME DE MENTHE, EARLY TIMES, FOUR ROSES, GOLD LABEL, GRAND MARNIER, HIRAM WALKER, JIM BEAM, KENTUCKY GENTLEMAN, LONDON DRY, MR. BOSTON, OLD CROW, OLD FITZGERALD, TIA MARIA, REBEL YELL, ROCKING CHAIR, SOUTHERN COMFORT, VIRGINIA GENTLEMAN, and WHITE LIGHTNING.

OUR KID
OUR MERCEDES
OUR MISS
OUR PRINCE
OUR _____
OUT 2 LUNCH
OUT 2 PASTURE
OUTA SIGHT
OUTA SITE
OUTA SPACE
OUTCAST
OUTFOXED
OUTGOING
OUTING
OUTLANDISH
OUTLANDOS
    D'AMOUR
OUTLAW
OUTLAW'S DREAM

OVERIJSSEL
OVERPOWER U
OVER SEAS
OVERTIME
OVERTURE
OVID
OWE NADA
OWLET
OWL
OWL HOOT
OWL OF ATHENE
OWN LIFE
OYSTER
OYSTER BAY
O ZONE

PACK RAT
PAC MAN
PADDLE KNOT
PADRE
PAEAN
PAEN
PAESANO
PAGAN
PAGE
PAGEN
PAGE ONE
PAGER
PAGET
PAGODA
PAID 4
PAID FOR
PAINE
PAINKILLER
PAINTED ELK

OWNER'S PROFESSION, VESSEL'S USE, TRADE NAMES

PAINTED PONY
PAIR-A-DICE
PAIR A DOX
PAIUTE
PAKA BAG
PAKER
PAL
PALACE TART
PALADIN
PALAMINE
PALATABLE
PALAU
PALAVER
PALAWAN
PALEFACE
PALE ROSE
PALETTE
PALEYMA
PALFREY
PALIMONY
PALISADE

PANDA
PANDA BEAR
PANDEMONIUM
PANDION
PANDORA
PANDORA'S BOX
PANIC
PANICLE
PANIC-KNOT
PANIOLO
PANJANDRA
PANJI
PANOPLY
PAN OUT
PANSHEE
PANSY
PANTHEA
PANTHER
PANTOMINE
PANTY RAID
PAPA

PARAMOUR
PARA MUTUAL
PARASOL
PARD
PAR EXELLLENCE
PARFAIT
PARFUM
PAR HASARD
PARIAH
PARI MUTUEL
PARIPASSU
PARIS
PARITY
PARK AVENUE
PARK RANGER
PARLAY
PARLOR BEAUTY
PARLOUS TOY
PARMA
PAR NONE
PARODY

*Cocktail time has also suggested: **APPLE JACK, BRASS MONKEY, BRONX, C.C. & WATER, GIN RICKY, HI BALL, HIGHLAND CREAM, HOT TODDY, MARGARITA, MINT JULIP, NIGHTCAP, OLD FASHIONED, RUM 'N COKE, SCREWDRIVER, SECOND MARTINI, SIDE CAR, SWIZZLE STICK,** or the all inclusive toasts: **CHEERS, DOWN THE HATCH, MUD IN YOUR EYE,** or **SALUTE.***

PALM
PALM BEACH LADY
PALM BREEZE
PALMER
PALMETTO
PALMIST
PAL O' MINE
PALOMINO
PAMELA
PAMIR
PAMPERED
PAMPERING
PAMPERO
PAN
PAN ACHE
PANACHE
PANAMA RED
PANATELA
PANCA
PANCHO 'N CISCO
PANCHO VIVA

PAPA BEAR
PAPAGO
PAPA'S BRIDE
PAPA'S LITTLE GIRL
PAPAW
PAPAYA
PAPER MOON
PAPILLON
PAPOOSE
PAPRIKA
PARABLE
PARACHUTE
PARA DICE
PARADISE
PARADISE FOUND
PARADISE SEEKER
PARADOX
PARAGON
PARAKEET
PARALLEL UNIVERSE
PARAMOUNT

PAROLEE
PARPMOUR
PARSEC
PARSEE
PARSLEY
PARSNIP
PAR T
PARTAKE
PARTAKER
PARTERRE
PARTI PRIS
PARTISAN
PARTLY MINE
PARTNER
PARTRIDGE
PARTY DOLL
PARTY GIRL
PARTY PERFECT
PARTY THYME
PARVENU
PASCAL

11

Animal, Vegetable Or Mineral:

Flora, Fauna & Natural Forces

Seashells, fishes, and other land or sea creatures, both real and imagined, are good selections for excellent boat names: ABALONE, ALBACORE, BADGER, BEAVER, BLOODHOUND, BUMBLEBEE, CHIPMONK, CORSAIR, COQUINA, DOLPHIN, DORADO, GAZELLE, GRASSHOPPER, HOBBIT, JACK, KANGAROO, KATYDID, MERMAID, NAUTILUS, NIGHT CRAWLER, OTTER, PENGUIN, PERIWINKLE, PLATYPUS, POMPANO, PUFF, PUFFER, RABBIT, RACCOON, SABLE, SAND DOLLAR, SCARAB, SCAMPI, SCOTCH BONNET, SEA ELF, SEAHORSE, SEA URCHIN, SILVER FOX, STARFISH, STINGRAY, SWORDFISH, UNICORN, WAHOO, WALLEYE, and ZEBRA.

In fact, a number of these creatures are chosen by sport boats because of their reputation, character traits, or predator activities: COBRA, COUGAR, GORILLA, JAGUAR, LYNX, MAKO, PIRANHA, POLECAT, SILVER FOX, WOLVERINE, and YELLOW JACKET.

FLORA, FAUNA & NATURAL FORCES

PASHA
PASSAGE
PASSAGE MAKER
PASSANT
PASSE
PASSING LANE
PASSIN' LANE
PASSION
PASSIOY
PATIENT WIFE
PATIENT _____
PATO
PATOIS
PATRICIA
PATRIOT
PATROLLER
PATRON O' POETS
PATSY

PAY ME
PAY MISTRESS
PAY OFF
PAZ
P D Q
PEACE
PEACE BASE
PEACEFUL
PEACEFUL JOURNEY
PEACEFUL PASSAGE
PEACEFUL PURSUIT
PEACEFUL SEAS
PEACEFUL _____
PEACE PIPE
PEACE SEAKER
PEACE SIGN
PEACE STAR
PEACE TREATY

PEASHOOTER
PECAN BELLE
PECCARY
PECKING ORDER
PECUSA
PEDIGREE
PEEKABOO
PEEPER
PEERLESS
PEE WEE
PEGASUS
PEGGOTY
PEGGY
PEGGY SUE
PEG LEG
PEIGNER
PEKING DUCK
PELE

---

*Flowers, nuts, fruit, and other flora have not missed the attention of mariners, and often combine with another meaning significant to the owner: **BLACK ORCHID, BUTTERCUP, CHESTNUT, CONIFER, FORSYTHIA, HIBISCUS, HYACINTH, JASMINE, JONQUIL, JUNIPER, LILAC, LILLY PAD, LOTUS, MAIDENHAIR, MAGNOLIA BLOSSOM, OLEANDER, ORANGE BLOSSOM, PALMETTO, PAPAW, PAPAYA, PRIMROSE, RED CEDAR, ROSE, SASSAFRASS, SEA LILLY, SEQUOIA, SHAMROCK, SNAPDRAGON, TAMARISK, THISTLE, TUMBLEWEED, TUTTI FRUTTI, WATER LILY, WILD FLOWER, and YELLOW ROSE.***

PATTA KAKE
PATTER
PATTY CAKE
PATTY O
PATTY PAY
PAU HANA
PAULA
PAULANI
PAUL BUNYON
PAUL REVERE
PAUNCHY
PAUSE
PAVLOV
PAVO
PAWNEE
PAWTUXET
PAYDAY
PAYDIRT

PEACE _____
PEACH BLUSH
PEACHES
PEACHIE
PEACH TART
PEACHY
PEACOCK
PEAFOWL
PEAHEN
PEALE
PEAL MI BELL
PEANUT
PEANUT BUTTA
PEANUTS
PEA POD
PEARL
PEARL OF _____
PEARLY GATE

PELICAN
PELL MELL
PELORUS
PENATES
PENCHANT FOR WIND
PENCHER
PENCIL POINT
PENDRAGON
PEN-DUICK
PENELOPE
PENGUIN
PENLIGHT
PENNING NOTHER
PEN 'N INK
PENNON
PENNSYLVANIA
PENNSYLVANIA 65,000
PENNSYLVANIA _____

PENNY ANTE
PENNY LANE
PENNY PINCHER
PENNYROYAL
PENSEE
PENSIVE DONNA
PENSIVE TAURUS
PENTUP ENERGY
PEON
PEONY
PEP PILLS
PEPPED UP
PEPPERMINT
PEPPERMINT LOUNGE
PEPPERY MISS
PEPPY FROG
PEPPERMINT TWIST
PEPPERS
PEPSI
PEQUOT

PERMANENT
   REVOLUTION
PERPLEXED
PERRY'S WINKLE
PER SE
PERSEPHONE
PERSEVERANCE
PERSIAN BLUE
PERSIAN CARPET
PERSIAN KITTY
PERSIAN LADY
PERSIAN NIGHTS
PERSIAN _____
PERSIMMON
PERSNICKETY
PERSONAL BEST
PERSONAL DREAM
PERSPECTIVE
PERSUADER
PERSUASION

PEYOTE SEEKER
PHAETHON
PHAETON
PHALAROPE
PHALLIC SYMBOL
PHANTASM
PHANTASY
PHANTOM
PHARAOH
PHAROS
PHASE ONE
PHAT
PHEADRA
PHEASANT
PHILADELPHIA
PHILADELPHIA
   FREEDOM
PHILLY
PHILTRE
PHLOX

Birds have been the voyager's friend and companion throughout history, and this association has influenced innumerable boat names: ALBATROSS, BALD EAGLE, BIRD, BOBOLINK, FALCON, GOLDEN PELICAN, GOOSE, HOMING PIGEON, HERON, KINGFISHER, KIWI, MAGPIE, ORIOLE, OSPREY, OWL, PELICAN, PIGEON, SEA BIRD, SEAGULL, SNOW GOOSE, STORMY PETREL, SUNBIRD, and TURTLE DOVE. We have also seen ENDANGERED SPECIES.

PERCHANCE
PER DIEM
PEREGRINE
PERFECTA
PERFECTION
PERFECT CADENCE
PERFECT DAYS
PERFECT DAZE
PERFECT LOVE
PERFECT RIVAL
PERFECT SPOUSE
PERFECT TOUCH
PERFECT WIND
PERFECT _____
PERFORMING ARTS
PERI
PERIL
PERILOUS RIVAL
PERILUNE
PERIWINKLE
PERKY

PER SUIT
PESCA
PESO
PET
PETALS
PETALUMA
PET BOAT
PETER VAN WINKLE
PETITE
PETITE CHATTE
PETITE MISS
PETREL
PETTED
PETTING TIME
PETTIT
PETUNIA
PET _____
PEU A PEU
PEWEE
PEYOTE
PEYOTE EATER

PHOEBE
PHOEBUS
PHOENIX
PHONIC SEAS
PHOSPHORUS
PHOTO COPY
PHYSICAL
PHYSICIAN'S CURE
PHYS ED
PHYSICS
PIBROCH
PICANTE
PICASSO
PICKENS
PICKLE
PICK OF LITTER
PICNIC
PIEBALD
PIECE A CAKE
PIECE O' CAKE
PIECE OF CAKE

FLORA, FAUNA & NATURAL FORCES

PIECE O' PI
PIECE O' PIE
PIECES
PIECES OF ATE
PIECES OF EIGHT
PIEDMONT

PILGRIMAGE
PILLOW
PILLOW TALK
PILOT
PILOTFISH
PIMENTO

PINK FLAMINGO
PINK LADY
PINKY
PINNACE
PINNACLE
PINON

PIED PIPER
PIGALLE
PIGEON
PIGGYBACK
PIG HEAVEN
PIKAKE
PIKI

PINA COLADA
PINAFORE
PINCHER
PINE KNOT
PINE NOT
PING
PINK CARNATION

PINTA
PINTO
PINWHEEL
PIONEER
PIONEER LADY
PIXIE
PIZAZZ

P J
P J'S
PLACEBO
PLACELESS
PLACIDA
PLAIN DAFT
PLAIN JANE
PLAN A
PLAN B
PLANE SCARED
PLANET ROAMER
PLANK 'N PROXY
PLANNER
PLASTIC DOLL
PLA TIME
PLATINUM
PLATO
PLATONIC LUV
PLATYPUS

PLUM BOLD
PLUMERIA
PLUM NICE
PLUNGER
PLURIPOTENT
PLUSH HORSE
PLUSH TOY
PLUTO
PLYMOUTH
P N L
P-NUT
PO
PO BOY
POCAHONTAS
POCO
POCONO
POCO A POCO
POCO POCO
POE

POLE STAR
POLESTAR
POLICE CAR
POLISHED LADY
POLISH PRINCESS
POLKA
POLLEN
POLLUX
POLLY
POLLYANA
POLLY'S CRACKER
POLLY WANNA
 CRACKA?
POLLYWOG
POLO PONY
POLY MER
POLYNESIA
POMONE
POMPANETTE

---

*Conditions of the nautical sky, sea, or sun, have been frequently noted by sailors: **CIRRUS, CLEAN AIR, CLOUDBURST, CRYSTAL WAVE, DARK MOON, ECLIPSE, EDDY, EMERALD SEAS, GENTLE BREEZE, GOLDEN PATH, GREEN FLASH, HEAT WAVE, MIDNIGHT SUN, MISTY, MOONBEAM, MOONGLOW, MONSOON, RAINBOW, RIPPLE EFFECT, RIPTIDE, ROGUE WAVE, SAPPHIRE SEAS, SEA MIST, SILVER CLOUD, SKY MAGIC, STARBURST, SUMMER FUN, SUNBEAM, SUNDOWNER, SUNNY, SUNSET, TIDAL WAVE, TSUNAMI, TWILIGHT TIME, WATERSPOUT, WAVE KING, and WHITECAP.***

PLAY
PLAYBOY
PLAYBOY'S _____
_____ PLAYER
PLAYFUL RENDITION
PLAYGROUND
PLAYMATE
PLAY PEN
PLAY ROUGH
PLAY TENDER
PLAYTHING
PLAY TIME
PLAY WID ME
PLEADES
PLEASED ME
PLEASER
PLEASURE
PLEASURE PALACE
PLUCKY

POEM OF ECSTASY
POETESS
POGO
POI
POILU
POINCIANA
POINT BLANK
POINT MAN
POIPU
POISED
POISON IVY
POKE
POKEY
POLAR BEAR
POLAR ESCAPADE
POLARIS
POLDER
POLECAT
POLE POSITION

POMPANO
POMPOM
PONCHAY
PONIARD
PONTCHARTRAIN
PONTIAC
PONY EXPRESS
POOH
POOH BEAR
POOH CORNER
POONTANG
POORHOUSE
POOR PEOPLE OF
 PARIS
POOU
POP ART
POP CORN
POPCORN
POPLAR

FLORA, FAUNA & NATURAL FORCES

POPPY	POWER TRIP	PRICAROON
POPPY POD	POWER _____	PRICE I PAID
POPSICLE	POWWOW	PRICELLA LANE
PORCH SWING	P POPSIE	PRICE OF EGGS
PORCUPINE	PRADO	PRICE TAG
PORPOISE	PRAETOR	PRIDE FILLED
PORQUOSIOUS	PRANA	PRIDE 'N PROMISE
PORSCHE	PRANAVA	PRIDE 'N SPIRIT
PORSCHE 911	PRANCER	PRIDE OF BALTIMORE
PORSCHE SPEEDSTER	PRANKSTER	PRIDE OF _____
PORSCHE TURBO	PRAY LUDE	PRIDE O' SEAS
POSADA	PRECISE	PRIDE RIDE
POSEIDON	PRESISION	PRIM
POSH	PREDATOR	PRIMA
P.O.S.H.	PREDATORS IMPULSE	PRIMA DONNA
POSH DAME	PREDAWN	PRIME CUT
POSITIVE	PRE DATER	PRIME INTEREST
POSSESSIVE LADY	PREDATOR	PRIME RATE
POST TIME	PREFECT	PRIME TIME

Descriptive wind terms, sometimes ominous in nature, are in keeping with vessels exposed to nature's elements: COOL BREEZE, ETHEREAL WINDS, FAIR WIND, GOD'S SPEED, HURRICANE, KIND WIND, LES 4 VENTS, NORDWIND, NORTHWIND, OCEAN WINDS, PERFECT WIND, PUFFA WIND, RIDE LIKE THE WIND, SECOND WIND, SECRET WIND, SQUALL, SUMMER BREEZE, TEMPEST, THE BREEZE AND I, TRADEWIND, TWISTER, TYPHOON, WHIFF, WHIRLWIND, WILLIWAW, WINDQUEST, WINDSONG, WINDY, WINDSWEPT, WISP, ZEPHYR, and not to exclude the sailor's lament: BLOWN OFFSHORE.

POTEEN	PRELIM	PRIMP 'N PREEN
POTENT WINNER	PRELUDE	PRIMROSE
POTION	PRELUDE TO LOVE	PRIMROSE PATH
POTLATCH	PRELUDE TRAIL	PRINCESS
POTLUCK	PREMIER	PRINCESS _____
POTOMAC	PREMIERE	PRINCE O' TIDES
POTOMAC FEVER	PREMISE	PRINCETON
POTPOURRI	PREMONITION	PRINGLE
POUILLY FUME	PREOCCUPIED	PRIORITE
POUND PUPPY	PRESERVER	PRIORITES
POUPEE	PRESIDENTE	PRISCILLA
POU STO	PRES MI BUTTON	PRISM
POWDER	PRES MI BUZZER	PRISMATIC
POWDER PUFF	PRETENDER	PRISM SEEKER
POWER	PRETTY BABY	PRISSY
POWERPAC	PRETTY PROMISE	PRISTINE
POWERFUL	PRETTY _____	PRIVATEER
POWERHOUSE	PREUX CHEVALIER	PRIVATE EYES
POWER TO SPARE	PREVENTER	PRIVATE WORLD

12

Come With Me To The Casbah:

Mystery, Intrigue & Fantasy

The exotic elements of nature, the infamous "witches' winds" from around the world inspire boat names: BISE (Swiss), CHINOOK (Canada & U.S.), FOEHN (Switzerland, Germany and Austria), LE MISTRAL (France), SANTA ANA (California), SHARAV, or HAMSIS (middle east), and SIROCCO (Italy).

PRIVILEGED CLASS
PRIZE
PRIZED
PRIZE WINNER
PROCYON
PRODIGAL

PROFITEER
PROF-N-TECH
PROFOUND
PROFOUND DELIGHT
PROFOUND ONE
PROFOUND RANGER

PROGENY
PROGRESS
PROGRESSIVE
PROJECTILE
PROLIXITY
PROMETHEUS

MYSTERY, INTRIGUE & FANTASY

PROMISCUOUS
PROMISE
PROMISE LAND
PROMOCEAN
PROMPT
PRONTO
PROPHESY

PROTOS
PROUD EAGLE
PROUD LADY
PROUD MARY
PROUD VIRGIN
PROUD _____
PROVACATEUR

PROXY
PRUDENCE
PRUDENT
PRUDENT PLEASURE
PRUDENT _____
PRY DWEN
PS

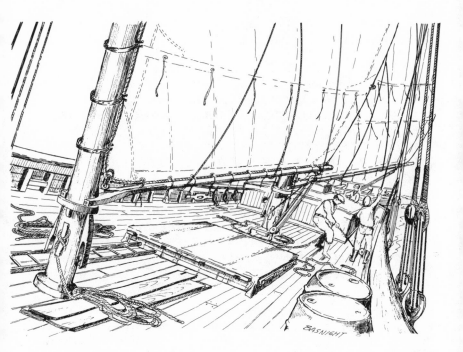

BASNIGHT

PROPHET
PROP WASH
PROSPECTER
PROTECTO
PROTECTOR
PROTEGE
PROTEST
PROTEUS

PROVED IT
PROVED MY POINT
PROVE IT
PROVEN ONE
PROVES MY POINT
PRÓVIDENCE
PROWESS
PROWLER

PSYCHE
PSYCHIC
PSYCHOACTIVE
PSYCHO
PSYCHO KILLER
PTARMIGAN
P'TIT LOUIS
P T L

P T O
PTOLEMY
PUA KAI
PUCK
PUEBLO
PUERILE LADY
PUFF
PUFFA WIND
PUFF DA MAGIC
   DRAGON
PUFFER
PUFFIN
PUFF'N STUFF
PUFF O' WIND
PUHI
PULSAR
PULSATING WAVES

PURE PLEASURE
PURE SILK
PURE _____
PURITAN
PURITY
PURPLE DREAMS
PURPLE HEART
PURPLE PASSION
PURPLE PEOPLE
   EATER
PURPOSE
PURSE STRINGS
PURSUER
PURSUIT
_____ PURSUIT
PUSS 'N BOOTS
PUSSYCAT

Q

Q C
Q CARD
Q E II
Q ME
Q TIP
QUACK
QUACK QUACK
QUACK QUACK DA
   FISHERMAN
QUADRILLE
QUADRANT

Some famous and fascinating names have resulted from an enchantment with magic, witchery and other mystical implications: ABRACADABRA, ALADDIN, BELIEVE 'N MAGIC, BEWITCHED, BLACK MAGIC, CASPER, CONJURER, DEMON, DOUBLE WHAMMY, ELUSION, GHOST, HOCUS POCUS, HOODOO, HOUDINI, LEPRECHAUN, MAGIC, MAGICIAN, MAGIC POTION, MANDRAKE, MR. WIZARD, MYSTIC, OCCULT LADY, OMEN, OUIJA BOARD, PALMIST, PHANTOM, POTION, PSYCHIC, SEA WITCH, SEER, SOOTHSAYER, SORCERER, SORCERY, SPECTRE, SPIRIT, SPOOK, SUPERSTITION, SURREAL, TALISMAN, THAT OLD BLACK MAGIC, VOODOO, VOODOO MAGIC, WAND, WARLOCK, WITCH, WITCHCRAFT, WITCH DOCTOR, WIZARD, and WIZARDRY.

PULSATOR
PUMPKIN EATER
PUNDIT
PUNJAB
PUNKIN SEED
PUNNED IT
PUNTA GORDA
PUNTER
PUPPETEER
PUPPY LOVE
PUPU
PURANAS
PURATIVE FLYER
PURDAH
PURE CLARITY
PURE HEAVEN
PURE PHYSICS

PUSSY GALORE
PUSSY WILLOW
PUSTEBLUME
PUTON
PUTTIN OUT
PUZZLE
PYEWACKET
PYLASTEKI
PYLOROS
PYRRHIC VICTORY
PYRRHUS
PYTHIAS
PYTHON

QUADRANTID
QUADROON
QUADROON WENCH
QUAGGA
QUAHOG
QUAI
QUAIL
QUAILIFIER
QUAILO
QUAIL'S NEST
QUAINT
QUAINT LIL LADY
QUAINT 'N NASTY
QUAISI FLIGHT
QUAISIMODO
QUAKE MAKER
QUAKE ME

MYSTERY, INTRIGUE & FANTASY

QUAKEN
QUAKING ASPEN
QUALEN
QUALIFIER
QUALIS REX
QUALITY MISS
QUAND MEME
QUANDRY
QUANTUM JUMP
QUARK
QUARREL SOME
QUARRY
QUARRY SEEKER
QUARTER BACK
QUARTER HORSE
QUARTER MOON
QUARTERS
QUARTERSTAFF
QUARTER TO THREE
QUARTO

QUEEN BESS
QUEEN ELIZABETH
QUEEN ELLY
QUEENFISH
QUEEN FREDERICA
QUEENIE
QUEEN MARY
QUEEN O'DIAMONDS
QUEEN OF BERMUDA
QUEEN O' CLUBS
QUEEN O' HEARTS
QUEEN O' LOVE
QUEEN O' SEAS
QUEEN O' SPEED
QUEEN _____
_____ QUEEN
QUELLE
QUENCHED MI DESIRE
QUENCH MI DESIRE
QUENGEL

QUEUE
QUIBBLE NOT
QUICHE
QUICK
QUICK DRAW
QUICKDRAW
QUICKEN
QUICKEN PULSES
QUICKIE
QUICKIE TRICKIE
QUICKMATCH
QUICK SAND
QUICKSAND
QUICKSILVER
QUICKSTEP
QUICKSTEPPIN
QUICK TEMPER
QUICK TIME
QUICK TRANSIT
QUID

Contributions suggested by dreams and other fantasies are: ALTERED STATES, APPARITION, ASTRAL, BUBBLE, DELUSION, ENTRANCED, FANTASY, IF ONLY, ILLUSION, MERRYTHOUGHT, MIRAGE, NARCOTIZED, NOTHINGLESS, PERSONAL DREAM, PHANTASM, PHANTASY, PIPE DREAM, PURPLE DREAMS, SEANCE, SEA SECRET, SECOND NATURE, SECRET PASSION, SWEET DREAMS, TECH DREAM, TELEPATHY, THESE DREAMS, TRANCE, TWILIGHT ZONE, UNREAL, and UNSEEN.

QUART R MOON
QUASAR
QUASH ALL
QUASH ALL TAKERS
QUASIMODO
QUASI BLAZE
QUASI DREAM
QUASI QUEAN
QUASI VIXEN
QUASTE
QUATSA LUCK
QUATSCHE
QUAVER NEVER
QUAVER NOT
QUAY LADY
QUEAN
QUEEN
QUEENA SCOTS
QUEEN BEA
QUEEN BEE

QUE PASA
QUERIDA
QUERIST
QUERULOUS CHILD
QUEST
QUEST BOUND
QUESTER
QUEST GUESS
QUESTION
QUESTIONING
QUEST LADY
QUEST O' DREAMS
QUEST O' GOLD
QUEST O' ISLES
QUEST O' LOVE
QUESTOR
QUEST QUELLER
_____ QUEST
QUETZAL
QUETZALCOATL

QUID NON
QUID PRO QUO
QUIEN SABE
QUIESCENCE
QUIESCENT LADY
QUIESCENT RIDE
QUIET CHAOS
QUIET COLORS
QUIET DANCER
QUIET DRAMA
QUIET DRIFTER
QUIET FRIEND
QUIET GRACE
QUIET MOMENTS
QUIET NOTE
QUIET SONGS
QUIET SPLENDOR
QUIETUDE
QUIET WINDS
QUIET _____

QUIK ENUFF
QUIK FREEZER
QUIK LEE
QUIK NESS
QUIK STEPPER
QUIK WIT
QUILL
QUIMPLE ONE
QUINCE
QUINTESSENCE
QUIPPE
QUIPPER
QUIPSTER
QUIRT
QUITE FRIENDS
QUITE GRACE
QUITE LONELY
QUITE NICE
QUITS
QUIT'N TIME
QUITYURBELLYACHEIN

R

RA
RAANI
R & B
R & D
RABBIT
RABBLE ROUSER
RABE
RABELAIS
RABID
RABID DOG
RACCOON
RACE HORSE
RACEHORSE
RACEM
RACE WINNER
RACHE

RAGNAR
RAGTIME
RAIDER
RAIL
RAIN BELLE
RAIN BO
RAINBOW
RAINBOW BUTTERFLY
RAINBOW CHASER
RAINBOW
  CONNECTION
RAINBOW LADY
RAINBOW LEGEND
RAINBOW MAIDEN
RAINBOW MEDICINE
RAINBOW MISS
RAINBOW PASSAGE
RAINBOW RANGER
RAINBOW RIDER
RAINBOW ROAD
RAINBOW SEEKER

Pirates, and seafaring terms provide a jaunty flair, incorporating added word-elements with significance to the owner or family: BILLY BONES, BILLY BUD, BLACKBEARD, BUCCANEER, CROSSBONES, DOUBLOON, JOLLY ROGER, PASSKEY, PASSION POTION, PIECES OF EIGHT, PIRATE, PIRATE'S COVE, TELL NO ONE, TREASURE HUNTER, and VISIONARY.

QUI VA LA
QUIVER
QUIVERING ARROW
QUIVERING DANCER
QUI VIVE
QUIXOTIC
QUIZ KID
QUIZZICAL
QUONDAM DREAM
QUONSET
QUORUM
QUOTE ME
QUOTIENT
QUO VADIS

RACING MACHINE
RACKETEER
RACONTEUR
RACY
RACY FOX
RADIANT
RADIANT WONDER
RADIATE
RADICAL
RADICAL RIDE
RAE
RAFALE
RAFEL
RAFFINEE
RAFFISH MISS
RAGA
RAGAMUFFIN
RAGA ONE
RAG DOLL
RAGE
RAGIN CAJUN

RAINBOWS FOREVER
RAINBOWS GOLD
RAINBOW TWINS
RAINBOW VOYAGER
RAINBOW WARRIOR
RAINBOW WOMAN
RAINBOW _____
RAINDANCE
RAINGIRL
RAINING
  BUTTERFLIES
RAINMAKER
RAINY DAY WOMAN
RAISE'N PAY
RAISING ZONE
RAISIN INDA SUN
RAISON D'ETRE
RAITE
RAJA
RAJAS
RAKETE

RAKISH	RARA AVIS	RAZORBILL
RALEIGH	RAREBIT	RAZOR'S EDGE
RAMBLER	RARE TREAT	RAZOR SHARP
RAMBLIN' MAN	RASALHAGUE	RAZZ
RAMBLIN' ROSE	RASCAL	RAZ-Z-BERRY
RAMBO	RASHER	RAZZBERRY
RAMBUNCTIOUS	RASPBERRY	RAZZLE DAZZLE
RAMONA	RASPUTIN	RAZZ MA TAZZ
RAMPAGE	RASSE	RAZZMATAZZ
RAMPANT LIONESS	RATE INCREASE	REACH BEYOND
RAMPANT WINNER	RATIFIED	REACHER
RAMPART	RAT RACE	REACH FOR IT
RAMPATAMPA	RAT RACE RESCUE	REACHIN' INN
RAMROD	RATTLER	REACH ME NOT
RAN	RATTLESNAKE	REACTIONARY
RANA	RATTLING TOY	REACTIVE MISS
RANA HINDU	RAUCOUS	READY
RANCHO MAR	RAUMLICH	READY MADE
RANDOM	RAUNCHY	READY MAID
RANDOM WIND	RAUWOLFIA	READY 'N RARING

> *Sometimes in the dramatic battle at sea between man and nature the elements became victorious, claming a wreck and sending off castaways to tell the tale. Some of the more infamous or notorious ones are: **BRINKBURN, CASTLEFORD, CITY OF CARDIFF, CIVET, G.I. JONES, H.M.S. ANSON, KHYBER, KING CADWALLON, MALTA, MINNEHAHA, MOHEGAN, PETRELLEN, PLYMPTON, SEINE, SUFFOLK, TABASCO, THAMES, T.W.LAWSON, and ZELDA.***

RANDY DANDY	RAVAGED	REAL DEAL
RANDY RASCAL	RAVAGER	REAL DELIGHT
RANDY TART	RAVELED	REAL ESTATE
RANGE RIDER	RAVEN	REAL FOCUS
RANGE ROVER	RAVENOUS	REAL IMAGE
RANI ANUPAMA	RAVENOUS GIRL	REALIST
RANSOME	RAVE RE VU	REALITY
RANT 'N RAVE	RAVERI	REAL JOY
RAPHAELO	RAVISHER	REAL TIMES
RAPID	RAVISHING BLOND	REASONS
RAPIDO	RAVISH YOU	REBATE
RAPID ONE	RAW NERVE	REBECCA
RAPID TRANSIT	RAW RHYTHM	REBEL
RAPIER	RAW TALENT	_____ REBEL
RAPPER	RAY CHASER	REBELLION
RAPPHANNOCH	RAY FISH	REBELLIOUS RIDE
RAPSCALLION	RAYS'N SUN	REBEL'S LADY
RAPTOR	RAY'S TOY	REBEL YELL
RAPTURE	RAZOR	REBIRTH
RAQUEL	RAZORBACK	REBOUND

13

Smooth, Slick & Saucy:

Dinghies, Multihulls & Other Size/Shape Relationships

DINGHIES, MULTIHULLS & OTHER SIZE/SHAPE RELATIONSHIPS

REBOUNDER
REBUS
RECEDE
RECESS
RECHERCHE
RECKLESS ABANDON
RECKLESS MONEY
RECLINER
RECLUSE
RECOIL
RECOLLECTIONS
RECOUP
RECOVERY
RECRUIT
RED BLAZER
RED BLOODED
REDBUD
RED C

RED CEDAR
RED DEER
RED DRAGON
RED E
REDEEMER
REDFIN
REDFISH
RED FOX
RED HEARTS
RED HERRING
RED HOTS
REDOLENT
REDOUTE
RED PEPPER
RED RAMBLER
RED RAPSODY
RED RAVEN
RED RIBBON

RED RIDER
RED ROOSTER
RED ROVER
REDSKIN
RED SKIES
RED SNAPPER
RED SPIDER
RED SQUIRREL
RED STAG
RED TAIL HAWK
RED TAPE
RED WAGON
REDWING
RED WINGS
RED WOLF
RED _____
REECHO
REED

Time and thought given to connecting the name of a tender or dinghy, in conjunction with the "mother ship" can give enormous satisfaction and stimulate many friendly exchanges with other boaters: BIG BEAR AND LITTLE BEAR, ETERNALLY and TIME AFTER TIME, FOOTLOOSE and FANCY FREE, I CAN SEE CLEARLY NOW and NOW, CHOCOLATE CHIP and COOKIE, CRESCENDO and HIGH C, LADY and LITTLE LADY, LOVE POTION and #9, KEEPER and THROWBACK, NEPTUNE'S FOLLY and NEPTUNE'S DOLLY, PATIENCE and YOUR ASS, SECOND MARTINI and OLIVE, THE MAGIC DRAGON and PUFF, THE RED BARON and SNOOPY, WHITE SPORT COAT and PINK CARNATION, or WAKE UP and LITTLE SUSIE.

REEL DELIGHT
REEL ESTATE
REETI
REFEREE NEEDED
REFINED LADY
REFLECTION
REFLECTIONS
_____ REFLECTIONS
REFLUX
REFORMED ME
REFUGE
REFUGEE
REGAL BEAST
REGALE
REGALIA
REGAL LADY
REGAL QUEEN

RELENTLESS
RELIABLE
RELIANCE
RELIANT
RELIEF
RELISH
REMAINDER
REMEDY
REMORA
REMOUNT
RENAISSANCE
RENAISSANCE LADY
RENCONTRE
RENDEZVOUS
RENDITIONS
RENE
RENEGADE

RERUN
RESCUE
RESOLUTE
RESOLUTION
RESOLVE
RESOURCE
RESPERINE
RESPITE
RESPOND
REST
RESTITUTION
RESTIVE
RESTIVE LADY
RESTLESS
RESTLESS SPIRITS
RESTLESS SWELLS
REST 'N PLACE

Very small boats, dinghies, tenders, or prams may carry a name influenced by the wee size of the vessel: ANCHOVY, CABOOSE, CHILD'S PLAY, COCKLESHELL, CRUNCH, DISCO DUCK, DWARF, ELF, ESCORT, FLIRT, FLYING FISH, FRISKY, GNAT, HIGH C, HUNKY DORY, LEGAL TENDER, LIGHTNING BUG, LIKEWISE, LITTLE SISTER, LOVE ME TENDER, MASCOT, MIMIC, MOSQUITO, PANFRY, PANTOMIME, PAPOOSE, PEANUT, PETITE, PLUCKY, PUCK, PUPPYLOVE, RIFT RAFT, RIPPLE, RUBBER DUCK, RUNT, SHADOW, S'KOSH, SEA EGG, SEA FLEA, SEA GERM, SEAPOD, SEA SEED, SLAVE, SMALL FRY, SPLINTER, TADPOLE, TAFFY, TAGALONG, TEARDROP, TEE NEE, TENDER MOTION, TIDBIT, TIPSY, TOM THUMB, TOO, TRINKET, VERBATIM, YUPPIE GUPPIE, and ZIT.

REGANDU
REGARDLESS
REGENT SEA
REGGAE MAN
REGINA
REGULUS
REHU MOANA
REINDEER
REJOICE
RELATIVE
RELATOR
RELAX 'N ENJOY
RELAX 'N RIDE
RELAXANT
RELAXED
RELEASE
RELEASED

RENEGADE GYPSY
RENEGADO
RENEGARE
RENEWAL
RENEGE
RENOIR
RENOWN
RENTED TIME
REPARTEE
REPLAY
REPORT CARD
REPOSE
REPUBLICIAN
REPULSE
REPUTE
REQUISITE
REQUITE

REST 'N REC
RESULTS
RESURGENT
RETALIATIONS
RETICENT
RETIREE
RETIREMENT
RETORT
RETREAT
RETROROCKET
RETTA
RETSINA
REVA
REVELATION
REVEILLE
REVELLER
REVENGE

DINGHIES, MULTIHULLS & OTHER SIZE/SHAPE RELATIONSHIPS

REVENGER
REVERIE
REVILLEZ
REVIVAL
REVIVED ME
REVOLVER
REVONOC
REWARD
REWARDING
REWARDING TIMES

RHODODENDRON
RHONDA
RHUBARB
RHUMBA
RHUMB LINE
RHYTHM
RHYTHMIC GRACE
RHYTHM METHOD
RIA
RIBALD

RIDDLE O' SEA
RIDDLE O' WINDS
RIDE 'EM
RIDE LIKE THE WIND
RIDE ON
RIDERS UP
RIDGE RUNNER
RIFF
RIFF RAFF
RIFF RAFT

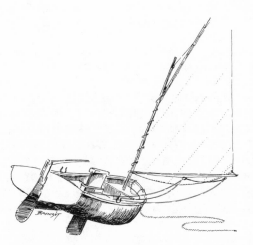

REX CAT
REYNARD
RHAPSADY
RHAPSODIC VISION
RHAPSODY
RHEA
RHETORIC
RHIANNON
RHINESTONE
   COWGIRL
RHINO

RIBBET
RICE PATTY
RICHARD CORY
RICH BITCH
RICH MAN'S TOY
RICH RIDE
RICK O' SHAY
RICKSHAW
RICO
RICOCHET
RIDDLE

RIFLEMAN
RIGAMAROLE
RIGEL
RIGHT BRAIN
RIGHT NOW
RIGHT ON
RIGHT S
RIGHT STUFF
RIGIL KENT
RILED
RIND

RING A DING
RINKIOHEN
RIO RITA
RIP 'EM UP
RIPE ORANGE
RIPPER
RIPPLE
RIPPLE EFFECT
RIP ROARING
RIPSAW
RIPTIDE
RISER
RISIBLE
RISIKO
RISING STAR
RISING SUN
RISING TIDE
RISK

ROBIN
ROBIN HOOD
ROBIN REDBREAST
ROBIN'S EGG
ROBIN'S NEST
ROBIN'S RAVEN
ROB ROY
ROBYN
ROCCA DI PAPPA
ROCK & ROLL
ROCK 'N RIDE
ROCKA ROO
ROCK AROUND THE
    CLOCK
ROCKER
ROCKET
ROCKING CHAIR
ROCKIN' HORSE

ROLLER
ROLLER CHASE
ROLLER CHASER
ROLLICK
ROLLIN
ROLLIN ALONG
ROLLING COASTER
ROLLING MACHINE
ROLLIN ROCKER
ROLLIN ROYCE
ROLLS 'N BUTTER
ROMANCE
ROMAN CANDLE
ROMAN CHARIOT
ROMANTIC EXPLORER
ROMANY
ROMANY STAR
ROMEO 'N JULIET

Trimarans and catamarans often carry descriptive names: ALLEY CAT,
BANANA SPLIT; BEAR CAT, BOBCAT, CAT 22; CATACLYSM;
CATALAC, CATALIST and CATALYST; CATAPILLAR (and
CATERPILLAR) CATASTROPHIC; CAT BALLOU, CAT CALL;
CATFISHER, CAT SASS, CATSKILL, CAT'S MEOW; CAT'S PAW,
CAT WALK, CHESHIRE CAT, DEUCE'S WILD, FRITZ THE CAT,
GARFIELD, HOW TRI I AM, KIDDY CAT, KIT KAT; KITTY CAT,
KOOL CAT, KRAZY KAT, ONE UP, SKIN A CAT, TABBY, THAT
CAT, THREE TIMES A LADY, TOM CAT, TOP CAT, TRIPLE
TROUBLE, TRI UMPH, TROPICAT, WIFE 'N TWO KIDS and
WILD KAT.

RISK IT ALL
RISQUE LADY
RISTRAS
RITE O' PASSAGE
RITI
RITUALS
RIVAL
RIVER
RIVERIE
RIVIERA
RIVER STYX
R N A
R N R
ROAD RUNNER
ROAD TO BLISS
ROAMER
ROARING 40'S
ROBERT E. LEE

ROCKIN' ROBIN
ROCK ME
ROCK 'N ROLL
ROCK STAR
ROCK THE BOAT
RODIN
ROE
ROGER
ROGUE
ROGUE LIONESS
ROGUE'S GALLEY
ROGUE'S ROOST
ROGUE WAVE
ROGUE WINDS
ROISTERER
ROJO
ROLE MODEL
ROLLA

ROMIN' KNOWS
ROMP
ROMPER ROOM
RONIN
ROOFTOP
ROOK
ROOKERY
ROOKIE
ROOM E
ROOM WITH A VIEW
ROOST
ROOSTER
ROOSTER TAIL
ROSA
ROSANNA
ROSCO
ROSE
ROSEAPPLE

ROSEBUD
ROSE O' SHARON
ROSE LEE
ROSEWOOD
_____ ROSE
ROSINE
ROSITA
ROSMARINE
ROSSIE
ROTSA RUCK
ROUGE
ROUGH RIDER
ROUGHRIDER
ROUGH WATERS
ROULETTE
ROUNDABOUT
ROUND AND ROUND
ROUND MIDNIGHT

ROYAL TERN
ROYALTY
ROYAL VALUE
ROY 'N DALE
ROY ROGERS
R S V
R S V P
RUBATO
RUBAYYAT
RUBBER DUCK
RUBBER DUCKIE
RUBE
RU BEE
RUBIC'S CUBE
RUBY
RUBY BABY
RUBY TUESDAY
RUCUS

RUNE
RUNNER
RUNNING BARE
RUNNING BEAR
RUNNY
RUNT
RUSH
RUSH BYE
RUSH HOUR
RUSH IN
RUSH OUR
RUSSARA
RUSSET
RUSTLER
RUTHLESS
RX
RYE
RYOKAN

Large and imposing ships frequently carry colossal or authoritative names: BISMARK, COLOSSUS, COMANDANTE, EMPEROR, EMPRESS OF CHINA, EXTRAORDINARY, GARGANTUAN, GENERAL LEE, GIGANTIC, HERCULEAN, IMPERATOR, LEVIATHAN, LUSITANIA, MAGNIFICIENT, MAJESTIC, MATADOR, MONARCH, NORMANDIE, PHARAOH, PRINCE, PRINCESS, QUEEN OF BERMUDA, QUEEN ELIZABETH, QUEEN MARY, REGAL QUEEN, REGINA, ROYALTY, SOVEREIGN, SPARTAN, STOUT FELLOW, SULTAN, TITANIC, TITAN, and WARLORD, On the other hand, one gleaming luxury yacht we've seen, complete with launches and helicopter pad, is LITTLE TOOT.

ROUND TABLE
'ROUND TUIT
ROUSTABOUT
ROVER
ROVER COME OVER
_____ ROVER
ROVIN MAN
ROVIN SEAS
ROVIN WAVES
ROWDY
ROWDY GIRL
ROWDY WENCH
ROWE BOAT
ROXANNE
ROYAL BONNET
ROYAL FLUSH
ROYAL MARINE
ROYAL SCAM

RUFFIAN
RUFFLES
RUFF 'N READY
RUFF RIDE
RUGBY
RUG RAT
RUMAWAY
RUMBA
RUMBLE
RUM 'N COKE
RUMORS
RUMPUS
RUMRUNNER
RUN
RUNAGATE
RUN AMOK
RUN AWAY
RUNAWAY

S

SABA
SABABU
SABBATICAL
SABER DANCE
SABI
SABIK
SABINE
SABLE
SABLEFISH
SABNAM
SABRINA
SABROSA

SABROSO
SACHEM
SACRAMENTS
SACRED COW
SACRED LADY
SACRED LOVE
SACRED PELE
SACRED PIPE
SACRED SEAS
SACRED WIND
SACRED WINDS
SACRISTAN
SADIE
SADIE HAWKINS
SAFAI
SAFARI
SAFE BET

SAILBAD THE SINNER
SAILFISH
SAILING LIFE'S FOR ME
SAILING STAR
SAILIN' SLAVE
SAIL LA VIE
SAIL ME
SAIL ON
SAIL ON 'N ON
SAILON SAILOR
SAILOR BILL
SAILOR'S CHOICE
SAILOR _____
SAIL UM
SAINT 'N SINNER
ST. AUGUSTINE
ST. CROIX

SALAAM
SALACIA
SALIDA
SALIRE
SALLY
SALLY FORTH
SALLY MAE
SALMO
SALMON
SALSA
SALTY DAWG
SALTY DOG
SALTY HUMOR
SALTY SEVEN
SALUDO
SALUTE
SALVAGE DUKE

Smooth, slick, streamlined, as if it can't be held back: CAN'T HOLD BACK, GLOSS ENDEAVOR, GRAPHITE, PEACHY, PRIM, SATIN DOLL, SHEER ROMANCE, SILK 'N SATIN, SILKEN WHISPER, SILKY, SUEDE, WET LOOK, and WHITE SATIN.

The name selected may be related to the class of boat involved. For example, oyster boats may carry a "racy" name, but most often they carry a two-part feminine name: ANNIE MAE, BECKY C., or MARGIE SUE. Owners of an extremely fast (and tender) class of Suicide sailboats maintain the spirt of the class with: AMEN, BELLADONNA, BLACK PLAGUE, COCAINE, DAVY JONES, FATALITY, IODINE, POISON IVY, and STRYCHNINE. In keeping with the theme, others could be: CUTTHROAT, EXTERMINATOR, RABID, RATTLER, TARANTULA, TERMINATOR, and VENOMOUS.

SAFEGUARD
SAFE 'N SECURE
SAFETY VALVE
SAFFLOWER
SAGA
SAGA SEAS
SAGAX
SAGE
SAGENHAFT
SAGES JOURNEY
SAGITTARIUS
SAGRES
SAGUENAY
SAHA
SAHIB
SAHNE
SAIL-ABOUT

ST. GEORGE
ST. HELENA
ST. JOHN
SAINT LO
SAINT LOUIS
ST. MARY'S
ST. PATRICK
SAINT PAUL
ST. THOMAS
ST. _____
SAKARA
SAKARAI
SAKI
SALA DE MAR
SALAMANDER
SALANA
SALDIEREN

SALVAGER
SALVATION
SALVE
SALVENTURE
SALVICTOR
SAMAASA
SAMARITAN
SAM CLAY
SAMIZDAT
SAMPLER
SAMPSON
SAMSAA
SAMSON
SAMT
SAMUEL B. ROBERTS
SAMUEL CHASE
SAMUEL N. MOORE

14

High Tech:

Racing, Fishing, and Competition

Owners and sponsors of fishing and race boats, and other charter or high performance craft, often select imposing names: ADVANTAGE, ADRENALIN, AROARA, BATTLEWAGON, BULLETPROOF, CONTENDER, CRISSCROSS, DRAGOON, EXHILARATED, FINALIST, FIREBOX, GUSTO, HOT FOOT, HOT PURSUIT, HOT MUSTARD, HOWLER, NERVELESS, OUTRAGEOUS, PERSONAL BEST, PISTOL, PRIZE WINNER, PURSUER, QUICKMATCH, RACY, RAMROD, REGARDLESS, REPULSE, RESTLESS, RIVAL, ROMP, SASY, SECRET FORMULA, SONIC BOOMER, SMOKE, SPRINT, STALKER, STAT, STRETCH OUT, STRIKE!, SUDDEN POWER, SURPRISES, THRILLER, THUNDERER, TOP KNOT, UNRIVALED, UPROAR, UTMOST, VIBRANT, VICTOR, VICTORIOUS, VITALITY, WINNER, WIPER OUTER, and WORTHY OPPONENT.

RACING, FISHING, AND COMPETITION

SAMUGA	SANTA LUCIA	SARX
SAMURAI	SANTA MARIA	SASHAY
SANCTUARY	SANTANA	SASSAFRAS
SANCTUM	SANTA PAULA	SASSY
SANDALS	SANTA ROSA	SASSY MAMA
SANDALWOOD	SANTEE	SASSY 'N FINE
SANDEFJORD	SANTEE SIOUX	SATINA
SANDERLING	SANTAI ENYU	SATIN DOLL
SAND DOLLAR	SANTUARIO	SATIN SEA
SAN DIEGO	SANUR	SATIRE
SAND MAN	SANZEN ICHINEN	SATIRIST

SAND PEBBLE	SAPA PAHA	SATISFACTION
SANDPIPER	SAPELO	SATORI
SAND PIPER	SAPPER	SATURN
SAND TRAP	SAPPHIRE SEAS	SATVA
SAN FRANCISCO	SARA	SATYRION
SANGUIN	SARACEN	SAUCY
SANGUINE	SARANGI	SAUDI PRINCESS
SANITY	SARASAN	SAUER DOUGH
SANSCRIT	SARATOGA	SAUMON
SANS SOUCI	SARGASSO	SAUNTER
SANSTED	SARI	SAUNTERER
SANS TERRE	SARIE	SAUSALITO
SANTA ANA	SARNACH	SAUTERNE
SANTA ELENA	SARONG	SAUVAGE

SAVAGE
SAVAGE GRACE
SAVAGE WARRIOR
SAVANNAH
SAVANT
SAVO
SAVOIR VIVRE
SAVOY
SAVVY
SAW BONES
SAWDUST 'N GLUE
SAWFISH
SAXON CHURL
SAY BYE BYE
SAYONARA
SAY SAY SAY
SAY SO
SAY YOU SAY ME
SCABBARD

SCAT
SCENARIO
SCENIC WAYS
SCHARFE
SCHATZ
SCHATZIE
SCHEDAR
SCHEDER
SCHEMER
SCHERZO
SCHEU
SCHNABEL
SCHNAPPS
SCHNELL
SCHOOLIE
SCHOOL MARM
SCHUSS
SCHWATZI
SCINTILLA

SCREAMING BANSHEE
SCREAMING EAGLE
SCREAMING EGO
SCREWDRIVER
SCRIBBLER
SCRIMSHAW
SCRUMPTIOUS
SCRUPLES
SCUFFER
S D I
SEA ABODE
SEA AIRS
SEA ANGLER
SEA BANDIT
SEABEAR
SEABELLE
SEABIRD
SEA BIRD
SEA BISCUIT

And who could forget: AGENT ORANGE, EAT MI WAKE, FAST COMPANY, FISH'N FOOL, FISH PEDDLERS, HAPPY HOOKER, HERE I COME, HIGH ENERGY, HOOKER TOO, ITZA SCREAMER, LEAN MEAN MACHINE, LIGHTNING ROD, MONKEY BUSINESS, OFFBEAT, PLAY ROUGH, QUACK QUACK DA FISHERMAN, QUICK TEMPER, REEL ESTATE, REEL DEAL, RICOCHET, ROUSTABOUT, SHOO-IN, SIZZLER, SLINGSHOT, SLOT MACHINE, SMART MOVE, SONIC NOK OUT, TALL COTTON, TOUR GUIDE, TRAX, TRUMP CARD, TUFF ACT, UNFORGETTABLE, WAR PATH, or WHOPPER STOPPER?

SCADS A DUCKETS
SCALAWAG
SCALLASA
SCALPER
SCAMP
SCAMPARE
SCAMPI
SCANDALOUS
SCANDALS
SCAN DA SEAS
SCANT SYMPATHY
SCAPEGOAT
SCAPEGRACE
SCAPEL
SCARAB
SCARLET
SCARLET O'HARA
SCARLETT
SCARLET TRIPTYCH

SCINTILLATION
SCIROCCO
SCISSORS
SCOOBY DOO
SCORPIO
SCORPION
SCOTCH BONNET
SCOTCH MIST
SCOTCH MISTY
SCOTCH 'N WATERS
SCOT FREE
SCOTFREE
SCOTT
SCOTT FREE
SCOUNDREL
SCOUT
SCRAMBLER
SCREAMER
SCREAMIN EAGLE

SEA BITCH
SEA BLISS
SEA BLOOD
SEA BOBBIN
SEABORNE
SEA BREEZE
SEABREEZE
SEA CALLER
SEACAT
SEA CAT
SEA CHARIOTEER
SEA CHASE
SEACHELLE
SEA CHIEF
SEA CHILD
SEA CLOUD
SEA CLOUDS
SEACLUSION
SEA CRUZE

RACING, FISHING, AND COMPETITION

SEACUP	SEA HARE	SEA PIGEON
SEA DANCER	SEA HAWK	SEA PINE
SEA DART	SEAHAWK	SEA PLUNDER
SEA DEUCE	SEA HORN	SEA POD
SEA DEVICE	SEAHORSE	SEA POACHER
SEADEVIL	SEA HOUSE	SEA PONY
SEADOG	SEA HUNTER	SEA QUEEN
SEA DOG	SEA IMAGE	SEAQUENCE
SEADRAGON	SEAIRA	SEAQUESTER
SEA DRAGON	SEA ISLAND	SEA RAMMER
SEA DREAMS	SEA KETTLE	SEA RAVEN
SEADUCER	SEA KING	SEARAVEN
SEA EGG	SEA KITE	SEARCHER
SEA ELF	SEA KITTY	SEA RED
SEA ESCAPE	SEAL	SEA ROAMER
SEA FAIRY	SEA LA	SEA ROBIN
SEAFARER	SEALANDER	SEA ROCKET
SEA FEATHER	SEA LASS	SEA ROSE
SEA FEVER	SEA LEC	SEA ROVER

Even more cunning or threatening, probably intending to intimidate racing or fishing opponents, we find: AVALANCHE, AWESOME, BLACKPOWDER, BLASTER, FURY, GANGSTER, GUNSLINGER, HAVOC, HOT DOG, MARAUDER, MONSTER, NO MERCY, ONSLAUGHT, PIT BULL, PREDATOR, PURPLE PEOPLE EATER, QUICK DRAW, RECOIL, RELENTLESS, RETALIATIONS, RIPPER, SCREAMER, SHOWDOWN, SLAMMER, STAMPEDE, STINGER, VENDETTA, VENGEANCE, VIGILANTE, WATER MOCCASIN, WILD BEAST, and XTRA HOT.

SEAFIRE	SEA LEGS	SEA SALVOR
SEAFLAME	SEALESTIAL	SEA SAW
SEA FLEA	SEA LEOPARD	SEA SCAMP
SEA FLOCK	SEA LEX	SEA SCANDAL
SEA FOAM	SEA LILLY	SEA SCANNER
SEA FOR TWO	SEA LION	SEASCAPE
SEAFOX	SEA LOVER	SEA SCOUT
SEA GARDEN	SEA MANTRA	SEA SECRET
SEA GAUL	SEA MIST	SEA SEED
SEA GERM	SEA MO SHUN	SEA SERPENT
SEA GIPSY	SEA NARIO	SEAS EXPRESS
SEA GOAT	SEANCE	SEA SHAPE
SEAGOER	SEA NETTLE	SEASHELL
SEA GORILLA	SEANIP	SEA SHEEP
SEA GRACE	SEA NYMPH	SEA SHELTER
SEA GUIDE	SEANYMPH	SEA SHIELD
SEAGULL	SEA ORCHID	SEA SISTER
SEA GYPSY	SEA O' SOLACE	SEA SKETCH
SEA HAG	SEA OTTER	SEA SKULL
SEA HAMMOCK	SEA PEARL	SEA SLEUTH

SEA SLICKER
SEA SLIDE
SEA SLUT
SEA SMARTS
SEA SNAIL
SEA SOLDIER
SEA SON
SEASONAL
    ADJUSTMENT
SEASONS IN THE SUN
SEA SOOTHER
SEA SOUNDS

SEA STROBE
SEA STROLLER
SEA SURE
SEA TACKER
SEA TEMPLE
SEA TEXTURES
SEA THREADER
SEA THYME
SEA TIGER
SEA TIGRESS
SEA TOY
SEA TRACS

SEA WHICH
SEA WINDER
SEA WITCH
SEA WIZARD
SEAWOLF
SEAZURE
SEA _____
SECLUDED 'N SILENT
SECLUSIVE SAIL
SECOND CHANCE
SECOND HAND ROSE
SECOND LOVE

SEA SNAKE
SEA SNARE
SEA SPLINTER
SEA SPRAY
SEA SPRITE
SEA SPROUTS
SEA STALLION
SEASTAR
SEA STAR
SEA STATION
SEA STEAD
SEA STEM

SEA TRAMP
SEA TREASURE
SEA TREE
SEA TREK
SEATTLE STEW
SEA URCHIN
SEA VEYOR
SEA WAGON
SEA WALKER
SEAWAY
SEAWEED
SEA WENCH

SECOND MARTINI
SECOND NATURE
SECOND REPEAT
SECOND START
SECOND WIND
SECOND _____
SECRECY
SECRET ESSENCE
SECRET FORMULA
SECRET PASSION
SECRET VU
SECRET WIND

RACING, FISHING, AND COMPETITION

_____ SECRET
SECULAR PASTIME
SEDA
SEDUCTION
SEE DOUBLE
SEE HERE
SEEKER
_____ SEEKER
SEELA
SEER
SEE SWING
SEE YA
SEE YA LATER
SEGLER
SEGOVIA
SEGUIDA
SEGURA
SEGURIDAD
SEHANS
SEHER

SENSUAL LADY
SENSUOUS TOY
SENSOR
SENTIMENTAL
  JOURNEY
SENTINEL
SENTINELLE
SENTRY
SEPARADA
SEPIA
SEPTEMBER SONG
SEQUEL
SEQUIN
SEQUINS
SEQUOIA
SERAFFYN
SERAGLIO
SERENA
SERENATA
SERENE

SEXY MAMA
SEXY MISS
SEXY THINGS
SEYCHELLES
SGT. MAJOR
SGT. PEPPER
SHABDIZ
SHABUMI
SHADES A BLUE
SHADOW DANCER
SHADOW DANCING
SHADOW MAKER
SHADOW _____
SHADY LADY
SHAKESPEARE
SHAKORI
SHALIMAR
SHAMAN'S LAIR
SHAMBALA
SHAMMY

... and even deadly force to help "do in" the opposition:
**_ANNIHILATOR, BLACK WIDOW, BLITZER, BOUNTY
HUNTER, BULLET, CANNIBAL, DEVASTATOR, ELIMINATOR,
EXTERMINATOR, GREAT WHITE, GUNNER, GUNSLINGER,
HAMMERHEAD, HEADHUNTER, KAMIKAZE, MACHINE GUN,
PROJECTILE, RABID, RATTLESNAKE, RAVAGER, RAVISHER,
SHOT GUN, SILVER BULLET, SLAM DUNK, SMOKING GUN,
SNIPER, SPEEDING BULLET, STANDARD MISSLE, STUN GUN,
STUNNER, TERMINATOR, ZAP, and ZIP GUN._**

SEKA
SEKU
SELENE
SELF CONCEPT
SELF DEFENSE
SELF-FULFILLMENT
SELF PORTRAIT
SELLAMA SUE
SEMILLION
SEMINOLE
SEMISHEER
SENATOR'S CLUB
SENGA
SENNET
SENORITA
SENSATIONAL
SENSIBLE
SENSE DESSERT
SENSITIVE WINDS
SENSUAL DELIGHT

SERINDIP
SERENDIPITY
SERENDY
SERENE CHANT
SERENITY
SERIOUS
SERIOUS MONEY
SERMON
SERRANA
SET BACK
SEVEN COME ELEVEN
SEVEN SEAS
SEVENTH HEAVEN
SEVEN YEAR ITCH
SEVERN
SEVERN RUN
SEVILLE
SEX APPEAL
SEX MACHINE
SEXY LADY

SHA MOI
SHAMPOO
SHAMROCK
SHANACHIE
SHANG RALA
SHANGRILA
SHARK
SHAR ON
SHARP MACHINE
SHARPSHOOTER
SHARP WIT
SHARRAV
SHAULA
SHAWNEE
SHEARWATER
SHEER ROMANCE
SHEIK
SHEILA
SHEKA
SHELDUCK

SHELLBACK
SHELLY
SHELTER
SHELTERED COVE
SHENANDOAH
SHENANIGAN
SHEREKHAN
SHERLOCK
SHERLUCK
SHERMAX
SHERPA
SHERRY
SHE'S A LADY
SHE'S MINE
SHIATSU
SHIH SHIH WU
SHIH TZU
SHIKAN MAKA
SHIKARA
SHI MA

SHOOTING STAR
SHOP AROUND
SHORT CIRCUIT
SHORT CUT
SHORTY
SHOT GUN
SHOTGUN
SHOT ME
SHOTOKU
SHOT O' RUM
SHOTOVER
SHOWBOAT
SHOWCASE
SHOWDOWN
SHOW OFF
SHREW TAMER
SHRIKE
SHRINKTA FIT
SHUJO SHO YURKU
SHURE THING

SIGNS O' DOVE
SIGUE MOLESTANDO
SIGUIENTE
SIHAATU
SIKONDI
SILENCE
SILENT FLOWER
SILENT THUNDER
SILHOUETTE
SILHOUETTES
SILKEN LADY
SILKEN WHISPER
SILK LUXURY
SILK 'N SATIN
SILK 'N STEEL
SILK PAJAMAS
SILK PURSE
SILK WORM
SILKY
SILLY GIRL

Then, to quietly throw opponents off guard, there are: ANXIOUS, BYSTANDER, COASTER, CREEPIN' CHARLIE, DECOY, HINDMOST, IDLER, LAGGARD, MOSEY, OUTFOXED, POKEY, SCAPEGOAT, SLEEPER, SLO POKE, SMOOTH TALK, SNAIL'S PACE, SUBTLE FOX, SURRENDER, TRO FEE, TROUNCER, TUCKERED OUT, UPSTART, WINSOME, WHIMPER, and YAWNER.

SHIMMERING ANGEL
SHIMMERING WATERS
SHINDIG
SHINE ON
SHINE ON SILVER
  MOON
SHINOLA
SHIP STAR
SHIRLEY
SHIVANI
SHIVERING MAIDEN
SHO
SHOESTRING
SHOGUN
SHOGON SHLEPPER
SHOJI
SHOKAIMOKU
SHOMON
SHOO-FLY
SHOOIN

SHUT OUT
SHUTTLE CRAFT
SHY CHILD
SHYLOCK
SIBLING
SIBYL
SIC 'EM
SIDECAR
SIDEKICK
SIDEREAL
SIDEWINDER
SIEMPRE
SIENNA
SIESTA
SIGMA
SIGMET
SIGNET
SIGNORA
SIGNOR G.
SIGNORINA

SILLY LOVE SONGS
SILLY SALLY
SILVA
SILVER APPLE OF THE
  MOON
SILVERBELL
SILVERBIRD
SILVER BULLET
SILVER CLOUD
SILVER ELK
SILVER FOX
SILVER HAWK
SILVER HEELS
SILVER KEEL
SILVER LABEL
SILVERLEAF
SILVER LINING
SILVERSIDES
SILVER SILVER
SILVER SPARKS

15

Off We Go:

Sports, Hobbies, Recreation, & Other Activities

A hobby, sport, or other favored activity, often suggests a potential boat
name perhaps with a flair of authority: ACES HIGH, BLACKJACK,
DEUCES WILD, HAM, HANG FIVE, HARDBALL, HEY RUBE,
HIGH MARK, HOYLE, JAVELIN, JOKERS WILD, LE MANS,
LONG SHOT, NATURALIST, ODDS MAKER, ONE EYED JACK,
OPTION PLAY, PACE SETTER, POLE POSITION, POLO PONY,
PUPPETEER, RIDERS UP, ROOKERY, ROULETTE, RUGBY,
SAFARI, SAND TRAP, SEASON TICKET, SEVEN COME ELEVEN,
SNAKE EYES, SNOOKER, SURE SHOT, TALLY DISH, TEE TIME,
TENSPEED, THE SAMURAI, TOUCHDOWN, and VICTORY
LANE. Some may incorporate all, or part of the owner's name.

SILVER SPURS
SILVER STAR
SILVERSWORD
SILVER _____
SIMBA
SIMON BOLIVAR
SIMPATICA
SIMPATICO
SIMPLE GIRL
SIMPLE LIFE
SIMPLE PLEASURE
SIMPLE STATEMENT
SIMPLE WINDS
SIMPLICITY
SIMPLICITY AT SEA
SIMPLY LUST
SIMPLY PERFECT
SIMPLY WUNDERFUL

SISI
SISIUTL
SISKA
SISKIN
SISSETON
SISU
SITA
SITAR
SITI
SITI URA
SITKA
SIXTEEN TONS
SIZZLE
SIZZLER
SIZZLIN SAL
SIZZLIN _____
SKANDIA
SKATE

SKIPPER'S SQUAW
SKIRMISH
SKITAWIT
SKITTISH FILLY
SKOIERN
SKOOKUM
SKORPIOS
SKUA
SKYBIRD
SKYBLAZER
SKY HAWK
SKYLARK
SKYLARKER
SKY MUSIC
SKY 'N SEA
SKYPORT
SKY SKOOTER
SLAM BANG

Pilots and crews have often named their airplanes in a manner appropriate to boats, like Lindberg's SPIRIT OF ST. LOUIS, and Sir Francis Chinchester's GYPSY MOTH, a manufacturer's name later applied to Chinchester's sailboats. Others we remember are: BREWERY WAGON, 'CISCO KID, CONTRAILS, FAST TRACK, FOLLOW ME, HELLDIVER, LADY LUCK, MY GIRL, PISTOL PETE, PROP WASH, SPITFIRE, SUSIE Q, THE RED BARON, THE SPRUCE GOOSE, THE TARHEEL TORNADO, THE GOLDEN GOOSE, VINDICATOR, and WIMPY. The influence of flying and airplanes probably created: AIRWAYS, FREQUENT FLYER, PLANE SCARED, and SPITFIRE.

SIN CERELY
SINEWY MISS
SING-A-LONG
SINGER
SINISTERRE
SINNER
SINN FEIN
SINSATIONAL
SIN SEMAFORO
SINSEMILLA
SIN SERVER
SIOUX
SIOUX MAIDEN
SIRENA
SIRIUS
SIROCCO
SIROCO
SIRU

SKATEBOARD
SKATER
SKEDADDLE
SKEPTIC
SKETCH
SKILL FILL
SKIMMER
SKIN A CAT
SKIN FLICK
SKINNED
SKINNY MINNIE
SKIPALONG
SKIPJACK
SKIPPER
SKIPPER'S CHILD
SKIPPER'S CHOICE
SKIPPER'S LADY
SKIPPER'S MISTRESS

SLAM DUNK
SLAM JAM
SLAMMER
SLAVE
SLAVE TO LOVE
SLEIGH RIDE
SLEEK GIRL
SLEEK 'N MEEK
SLEEPER
SLEEPWALKER
SLEIGH RIDE
SLEIGHT TOUCH
SLENDER LADY
SLENDER MISS
SLEUTH
SLIDER
SLIM
SLINGER

SPORTS, HOBBIES, RECREATION, & OTHER ACTIVITIES

SLING SEAT
SLINGSHOT
SLINKY
SLIPAWAY
SLIPPERIEST
SLIPPIN OFF
SLIPSTREAM
SLOE EYED
SLOPOKE

SMALL WORLD
SMART ALEC
SMART MOVE
SMART STUFF
SMILER
SMILES
SMILING DOC
SMOKE
SMOKER

SNALLYGASTER
SNAPDRAGGIN
SNAPDRAGON
SNAP DRAGON
SNAPPER
SNAPPY
SNAP SHOT
SNAPSHOT
SNARE

SLO ROLLER
SLOT MACHINE
SLOW DANCE
SLUMBERJACK
SLUMLORD
SLY FOX
SLYPH
SMACKWATER JACK
SMALL FRY
SMALL WERL

_____ SMOKE
SMOKING
SMOKING GUN
SMOOTH OPERATOR
SMOOTH TALK
SMUGGLER
SNAIL DARTER
SNAIL'S PACE
SNAKE
SNAKE EYES

SNARK
SNATCH
SNICKERS
SNIDELY WHIPLASH
SNIKE
SNIPE
SNIPER
SNOOPY
SNOOZEN
SNOOZIN

SNORRE
SNOWDROP
SNOWFLAKE
SNOW GOOSE
SNOWGOOSE
SNOW LEOPARD
SNOW SQUALL
SNOW WHITE
SNOW _____
SNUFFBOX
SNUGGLE
SNUGGLER
SNUGLY
SOARING
SOBRENATURAL
SOBRINA
SOEUR
SOFARSOGOOD

SOLITARIO
SOLITARY
SOLITARY BIRD
SOLITUDE SETTING
SOLOIST
SOLON
SOLONG
SOLOQUY
SOLO VOYGER
SOLTERO
SOLUTION
SOLUTION MAKER
SOI
SOMERS
SOMETHIN'
SOMETHING SEA
    REOUS
SOMETHIN' STUPID

SONO-MAMA
SONRISA
SOO FAST
SOOO FINE
SOOK
SOOTHING
SOOTHING MOTIONS
SOOTHING WAVES
SOOTHSAYER
SOOTY TERN
SOPHIA
SOPHISTICATED LADY
SOPRANINO
SOQUI
SOQUOIAH
SO RARE
SORCERER
SORCERESS

Track racing, an attachment to horses, or other racing interests, may prompt a suitable name: BLACK FILLY, COLT, CRITICS CHOICE, DAILY DOUBLE, FAST TRACK, HIGH ROLLER, HORSE WITH NO NAME, LOGICAL CHOICE, LUCKY CHOICE, MAN O' WAR, MOONLIGHT, PAINTED PONY, PALOMINO, PARI MUTUAL, PINTO, POST TIME, RACEHORSE, RANGLER, RUSTLER,SCOUT, SEA STALLION, SILVER SPURS, SKITTISH FILLY, STARLIGHT, SUNDANCER, TALLY HO, TIPSTER, TRAVELLER, TRIGGER, TROTTER, UNBEATEN, UNBRIDLED, WILD HORSE, WINNER'S CHOICE, WINNER'S CIRCLE, and WINNER'S PRIDE.

SO FINE
SOFT SELL
SOI
SOI DISTANT
SOINTY
SOIRE
SOIREE
SOJOURN
SOLACE
SOLACE SEA
SOLAMENTE
SOLANO
SOLARELLE
SOLAR SPY
SOLERI
SOLIDAGE
SOLILAI
SOLITAIRE

SONA
SONADORA
SONATA
SONG
SONGBIRD
SONGKRAN
SONG SUNG BLUE
SONG THRUSH
_____ SONG
SONIC BOOM
SONIC BOOMER
SONIC KNOCKOUT
SONIC LIGHT
SONIC NOK OUT
SONIC WAVES
SONNENBERST
SONNY
SON OF A GUN

SORCERY
SO REAL
SORTÉ
SORTIE
SO SO
SOTICA
SOTIE
SOTTO VOCE
SOUCRE
SOUFIRE
SOUFRIERE
SOUL A NIGHT
SOUL CATCHER
SOUL DANCER
SOUL MAN
SOUL RITES
SOUL-STIRRER
SOUND 'N SIGHT

SPORTS, HOBBIES, RECREATION, & OTHER ACTIVITIES

SOUND OF MUSIC
SOUND O' SEA
SOUNDSCAPE
SOUNION
SOUSHAY
SOUTH AUSTRALIA
SOUTH CAROLINA
SOUTH DAKOTA
SOUTHERLY
SOUTHERN BELLE
SOUTHERN BRIDE
SOUTHERN COMFORT
SOUTHERN CROSS
SOUTHERN DRAWL
SOUTHERN EXPOSURE
SOUTHERN FLOWER
SOUTHERN GIRL
SOUTHERN ISLES
SOUTHERN MAID
SOUTHERN NIGHTS

SPANISH EYES
SPANISH HARLEM
SPAULDING
SPARE CHANGE
SPARE TIME
SPARKLE
SPARKLE FARKLE
SPARROW HAWK
SPARTAN
SPAT
SPEARFISH
SPEARHEAD
SPEARPOINT
SPECIAL EDITION
SPECIAL LADY
SPECIAL MISS
SPECIAL _____
_____ SPECIAL
SPECTRA
SPECTRE

SPINACH
SPINDRIFT
SPINDRIFTER
SPIRAL
SPIRIDE
SPIRIT
SPIRIT DANCER
SPIRIT O' ADVENTURE
SPIRIT OF AMERICA
SPIRIT OF JOY
SPIRIT OF ST. LOUIS
SPIRIT OF _____
SPIRITUAL APPROACH
SPIRITUAL MUSE
_____ SPIRIT
SPITEFUL
SPITFIRE
SPIZZ
SPLASHDANCE
SPLENDID

Practically any means of propulsion is appropriate and will apply, perhaps to one type of boat more than to another: AIR EXPRESS, CHARIOT, HOT ROD, NEPTUNE'S EXPRESS, POGO, POLICE CAR, PONY EXPRESS, PORCH SWING, QUIK ENUFF, RAPID TRANSIT, RICKSHAW, ROCKER, ROCKET, ROLLING COASTER, ROMAN CHARIOT, SEA STROLLER, SHUTTLE CRAFT, SKATEBOARD, SKATER, SLEIGH RIDE, SPACE BUGGY, SUPER SCOOTER, TEETER TOTTER, THE LOCO-MOTION, TORPEDO, WATER BED, and YELLOW SUBMARINE.

SOUTHERN PRIDE
SOUTHERN QUEEN
SOUTHERN REBEL
SOUTHERN SAVAGE
SOUTHERN SEA
SOUTHERN SEAS
SOUTHERN STARLET
SOUTHERN WAVE
SOUTHHAMPTON
SOUTHSEAS
SOUTH SEAS
SOUTH WIND
SOVEREIGN
SOVRAN
SOW 'N REAP
SPACE BUGGY
SPACE CASE
SPACE JOURNEY
SPACE SOJOURNER
SPACEY

SPECTRUM
SPECULATOR
SPEED
SPEEDING BULLET
SPEED LIMIT
SPEEDWELL
SPEEDWELL OF HONG
  KONG
SPEEDWORK
SPEEDY
SPEEDY LASS
SPHINX
SPICA
SPICE
SPICEFINCH
SPIDER
SPIDER PEOPLE
SPIDER'S SPELL
SPIDER'S WEB
SPIKE

SPLENDOR
SPLENDOR O' SEAS
SPLINTER
SPLIT IMAGE
SPOILED BRAT
SPOILED ROTTEN
SPONTANEOUS
SPOOK
SPOONBILL
SPORTIN' LADY
SPORTSMAN
SPORTY
SPOT
SPOTTED HAWK
SPOTTED HORN
SPRAY
SPREAD EAGLE
SPRIG
SPRIGHTLY
SPRING

SPRING ARDOR	STAG PARTY	STARMUSIC
SPRING CHICKEN	STAINLESS	STAR OF _____
SPRING FEVER	STAKLER	STAR O' SEA
SPRING FLING	STAMINA	STAR PAL
SPRING LUST	STAMPEDE	STAR PEACE
SPRING RITES	STANDARD MISSILE	STAR QUALITY
SPRINGER	STANDOUT	STARRING
SPRING BOK	STANDPOINT	STARRY NIGHTS
SPRING LOADED	STAR	STARS & STRIPES
SPRING TIDE	STAR A MINE	STARSHIP
SPRING _____	STARBORN	STARSTRUCK
SPRINT	STARBOUND	STARTIN OVER
SPRINTER	STAR BRIGHT	STARTLED
SPRITE	STARBURST	STAR _____
SPRUCE	STARCASTER	_____ STAR

Names expressing practically any type of activity or otherwise indicating speed or motion are also well-chosen: BUSYBODY, CAKEWALK, CAN'T STOP, CURRENT AFFAIR, DARTER, DASH, DEAD HEAD, DISTURBANCE, FREEWHEELING, GETTIN' IT ON, GOOD VIBRATIONS, GROOVIN', GUSTO, HARD KNOCKS, HIJINKS, HI VELOCITY, HOT PURSUIT, HUSTLE, JOLT, LICKETY SPLIT, LIVELY LADY, LOOKS FAST, MAJOR MOTION, MERRY ROVER, OOPSY DAISEY, NIP 'N TUCK, PASSING LANE, PRANCER, PROWLER, PULSATOR, PURSUIT, QUICK TIME, RAMBLIN' MAN, RAMBLIN' ROSE, RESTLESS, RIGAMAROLE, ROLLICK, RUNAWAY, SAUNTERER, SCAT, SEA CHARIOTEER, SHOP AROUND, SKEDADDLE, SKIPALONG, SLITHER, SPONTANEOUS, STRIDER, SUNCHASER, SURFACE ACTION, SWEEP UP, SWIFTY, TOSSIN' AND TURNIN,' TRAVEL AGENT, TRAVELING CIRCUS, TRAVELIN' MAN, TREPIDATION, UNSHAKEN, VENTURER, VIBES, WANDERER, WANDERLUST, WHAT'S SHAKIN, and ZIP ALONG.

SPRY FRY	STAR CHILD	STAT
SQUALL	STAR CLOUD	STATE OF MAINE
SQUARED UP	STAR CRUISER	STATE OF MIND
SQUAW	STARCRUISER	STATE OF _____
SQUIRREL	STARDOM	STATESMAN
SQUERAROLI	STARDUST	STATUS QUO
S.S. MINNOW	STARFIRE	STAYING ALIVE
S SUGAR	STARFISH	STEADFAST
STABILO BOSS	STAR FORCE	STEADY GIRL
STABLE PONY	STARGAZER	STEAK 'N KIDNEY
STACEY	STAR GAZER	STELLA
STACY	STARK	STELLAR VOYAGE
STAGE FRIGHT	STARLET SCARLET	STELLAR VOYAGER
STAGE STRUCK	STARLIGHT	STELLER
STAGGER LEE	STARLING	STELLER AMBITION

16

The ABC's Of It:

Playing With Words & Letters

Slang expressions, often retained from another geographical location, or another time and place, presumably have personal significance to the owner: *A OVER T, BATTLER, BIG BANANA, BONKERS, CHILD'S PLAY, DUCK SOUP, FAIR DINKUM, FLYING A, GOLLIWOG, HOMEWORK, HOT TICKET, KUSH TUSH, ONION PATCH, PIECE A CAKE, RANDY TART, ROCKA ROO, 'ROUND TUIT, SCRUMPTIOUS, SNAFU, THINK AGAIN, TOO MUCH, UNDIES, UPTOWN, WHAT A GAS, WING IT, and WORK O' ART.*

The trend toward vanity license plates on automobiles may carry over to boaters: *BYE YAL, FAROUT, FLYBY, IBBAC, IMB4U, I O R, RACEM, SMOKIN, SUGGA, WISE 1., WEGON, and WIS DOM.*

STEP AHEAD	STOCK PORTFOLIO	STRAY HEIFER
STEPMOTHER	STOCKS 'N BONDS	STREAKER
STEP ON IN	S T O L	STREETGANG
STEPPIN' OUT	STONE SOBER	STRENGTH
STEREO	STONES THROW	STRESS RELIEF
STERLING	STOOP	STRETCH OUT
STERLING HAYDEN	STOP ME	STRICTLY BIZZ
STICKLEBACK	STORK	STRICT SENSE
STICKS	STORMAWAY	STRIDER
STILL CRAZY	STORMY PETREL	STRIKE
STILL SEA	STORMY WEATHER	STRIKER
STILL THE BEAR	STORNAWAY	STRINGFELLOW
STILLWATER	STORY TELLER	STROBE LIGHT
STING	STOUT FELLOW	STROLLEE
STINGER	STOWAY	STRONGBOW
STINGRAY	STOWAWAY	STRONGHOLD
STLL CRAZY	STRAIGHT ARROW	STUBBORN MISS
STOCKINSTUFFER	STRAT	STUCK UP

STUD FEES
STUNG
STUN GUN
STUNNER
STUNNING
STUNNING DAMSEL
STUPA
STURDY BEGGAR
STURDY GIRL
STURGEON
STURTEVANT
STUTTGART
STYX
SUAVE
SUBLIME
SUB PLOT
SUBTLE 'N SPICY
SUBTLE BABY
SUBTLE FOX

SUITE
SUITE FOR ONE
_____ SUITE
SUITOR
SUKA
SUKIYAKI
SULTAN
SULTANA
SULTANATE
SULTRY
SULU
SUMERU
SUMMA
SUMMARY
    JUDGEMENT
SUMMA WINDS
SUMMER BREEZE
SUMMER FUN
SUMMER MEMORIES

SUNDANCER
SUN DANCER
SUNDAE _____
SUN DAY
SUN DEVIL
SUN DOG
SUNDOWNER
SUNDOWN KID
SUNDOWN POWWOW
SUNDREAMER
SUNDROP
SUNFISH
SUNFLOWER
SUN FUN
SUNGLO
SUN GO DOWN
SUNMAID
SUN 'N MOONGLO
SUNNY

Newly coined words, technical words, and modern expressions are AVANT-GARDE and provide modern perspective and expression for a boat owner: AWESOME, FASTER ACCESS, CHEAP THRILLS, CONSTANT, COP OUT, CRITICAL MASS, CUTTING EDGE, FUSION, HARDCORE, HIGH TECH, HOT LINE, HUMONGOUS, INTERFACE, LEADING EDGE, OFF LINE, ON LINE, PIZZAZZ, PRIME TIME, RERUN, RIGHT ON, RUBIC'S CUBE, RUNAWAY, SHORT ORDER, STEP AHEAD, SYNERGISM, TAKE OUT, THE EDGE, THIRD WORLD, TIME WARP, TRENDY, UP FRONT, WHITE OUT, WIPE OUT, and YUPPIE'S DREAM.

SUBTLE PLOT
SUBURBIA
SUCCESS
SUCH CLASS
SUCH LUCK
SUCK EGGS
SUDDEN POWER
SUEDE
SUGAR
SUGAR DADDY
SUGAR 'N SPICE
SUGAR PLUMB
SUGAR SHACK
SUGARSHACK
SUGAR, SUGAR
SUGARTIME
SUGGA
SUHAILI
SUHALL

SUMMER SPECIAL
SUMMER RECESS
SUMMER ROSE
SUMMERTIME
SUMMER WIND
SUMMER _____
_____ SUMMER
SUM TOTAL
SUM TOY
SUNBEAM
SUN BEAR
SUNBIRD
SUNBORN
SUNBORNE
SUNBURST
SUNCHASER
SUNDAE
SUNDAE LOVERS
SUNDANCE

SUNNY SIDE UP
SUNRAYS
SUN RAYS
SUNROOF
SUN RUNNER
SUNSEA
SUN SESSIONS
SUNSET
SUNSET DANCER
SUNSET SEEKER
SUN SHADOWS
SUNSHIP
SUNSHOWER
SUN SONGS
SUN SPIRITS
SUN STROBE
SUNTANNED
SUNYA
SUN _____

PLAYING WITH WORDS & LETTERS

SUPERB DOLLY
SUPER CHIEF
SUPER DUPER
SUPER EIGHT
SUPER ENCORE
SUPER FINE
SUPERFLEA
SUPERFOX
SUPERIOR
SUPER MISS

SURE FIRE
SURE NUFF
SURE SHOT
SURE THING
SURE TURN
SURFACE ACTION
SURFBIRD
SURF CITY
SURF SIDE
SURGEONS SKIFF

SUTA
SUTRA
SUVARUGE
SUZANNE
SVAALU
SVELTE
SWAG
SWAIN
SWAMI
SWAN

SUPER NICE
SUPER SAILOR
SUPER SCOOTER
SUPERSKIFF
SUPERSTAR
SUPERSTITION
SUPERTRAMP
SUPER _____
SUPPLE MISS
SUPRA
SUPREME COURT
SURA
SURE CURE

SUR MER
SURPRISE
SURPRISES
SURREAL
SURRENDER
SURSEA
SUSIE B
SUSIE GREY
SUSIE Q
SUSIE WONG
SUSPECT
SUSSUDIO
SUSURRANT

SWALLOW
SWALLOWS NEST
SWANSONG
SWAN SONGS
SWAP 'N MEET
SWARTHY
SWASHBUCKLER
SWEDE
SWEEP UP
SWEET 16
SWEET AGNES
SWEET AND GENTLE
SWEET BASIL

SWEETBRIAR
SWEET DOMAIN
SWEET DREAMS
SWEETGUM
SWEETIE
SWEETIE PIE
SWEET MAMA
SWEET MOMA
SWEET 'N NASTY
SWEET OKOLE
SWEET P
SWEETS
SWEET SAVAGE
SWEET SUE
SWEET SOLITUDE
SWEET SPIRIT
SWEET THING

SWORD DANCE
SWORDFISH
SYBARIS
SYLVAN NYMPH
SYLVIA
SYMBIOSIS
SYMBIOTIC
  RELATIONSHIP
SYMMETRY
SYMPHONY
SYNAPSE
SYNCHRONICITY
SYNCOPATION
SYNERGISM
SYNONYM
SYNSONIC
SYNTAX

TABOR BOY
TABRIZ
TACH YON
TACITURN
TACKFUL
TACKLE BOX
TACKLER
TACOMA
TACO VENDOR
TACTFUL
TADPOLE
TAEPING
TAFAATU
TAFFY
TAG
TAG ALONG
TAGEBUCH

Skillful word or letter substitution involving proper names and/or other terms, combine to create successful and interesting names:
BASSACKWARDS (with last "S" backwards), BAY GULL, CAT'S PAUSE, ENTER LEWD, ERRONEOUS ZONE, E Z PEACE, FIASCO (with upside down "A"), HAIRBRAINED or HAREBRAINED, HOT RUDDERED BUM, LEAN CRUISINE, MO SHUN, MOSION (or MOSHUN), ODD A SEA, OFF MI ROK R, PAR T, PER SUIT, QUARREL SOME, QUARTER BACK, RUFF or RUF, SAIL LA VIE, SEA DUCE, SEA FOR TWO, SEA SAW, SEASURE (SEA SURE or SEAZURE), SLUMBERJACK, SUNDAE LOVERS, SWELL BOUND, TIMBUK II, TOMATO SLOOP, TRUE LUFF, U FOR ICK, VAN GO, WINNER WINDS, WIN SWEPT, WINWANWON, WOBEGONE DAZE, WRECKLESS or RECKLESS, WRENEGADE, WRITE ON, and YANKIE for YANKEE.

SWEET WATERS
SWEETWATERS
SWEET _____
_____ SWEET
SWELL BOUND
SWIFT
SWIFT CURRENT
SWIFT DISPATCH
SWIFT PASSAGE
SWIFTSURE
SWIFT WINDS
SWIFTY
SWINDLER
SWING 'N SWAY
SWISS WATCH
SWIZZLE STICK
SWOOZY

SYNTHESIS
SYNTHESIZER
SYREN
SYSTOLE

T

TAAS
TABALA
TABASCO
TABBY
TABITHA
TABLEAU
TABLOID
TABOO

TAGLICH
TAGLIONI
TAHAA
TAHITI
TAHITIAN VAHINE
TAHITI YELLOW
TAHOE PRINCESS
TAI CHI
TAIGA GIRL
TAILOR MADE
TAIL SPINNER
TAIPI
TAJ MAHAL
TAKA CHANCE
TAKE FIVE
TAKE ME
TAKE OFF

PLAYING WITH WORDS & LETTERS

TAKE OUT	TANAGER	TAR BABY
TAKE WING	TANDEM	TARDAR
TAKING CARE	TANE	TARDY
TAKU	TANGAROA	TAREA
TAKUVA	TANGELO	TARGE
TA LA	TANGENT	TARGET
TALA	TANGERE	TAR HEEL
TALANTA	TANGERINE	TARI
TALEBEARER	TANGIER	TARIFF
TALE SPINNER	TANGLE	TARL
TALIGUN	TANGO	TARMENEL
TALISMAN	TANIA AEBI	TARO
TALIESIN	TANIWHA	TAROA
TALK'S CHEAP	TAN PRONTO COMO	TAROT
TALLADEGA	TANQUERAY	TAROT CARDS
TALLAWA	TANSTAAFL	TARPON
TALL COTTON	TANSY	TARRAGON
TALLY DISH	TANTA	TARROGON
TALLY HO	TANTALIZER	TARRY NOT

Along the same lines, but possibly suggesting bolder statements, we've seen other imaginative and humorous names containing substitutions: CENT, SCENT for SENT; BARE or BEAR, COARSE or COURSE, DAZE for DAYS, HINESIGHT for HINDSIGHT, HIPNOSIS for HYPNOSIS, KNOTICAL or NAWTICAL for NAUTICAL; KORKER for CORKER, LICKER for LIQUOR, MADE or MAID, MALE for MAIL, NAUGHTY (or NAUTI) for NAUTY, NAVEL for NAVAL, NOT or KNOT, OLIMPICS for OLYMPICS, PIECE for PEACE, TAIL for TALE, WEAKEND for WEEKEND; WHETHER or WEATHER; and WITCH for WHICH.

TALLYWHACKER	TANTALUS	TARTAN
TALMUDIC	TANTE	TARTAR
TALOFA	TANTRA	TARUS
TALU DANDI	TANTRUM	TARWATHIE
TAL VEZ	TANZIN	TARZAN
TAMALE	TAO	TARZAN'S JANE
TAMALPAIS	TAOIST	TASHI REETI
TAMAR	TAOS	TASKMASTER
TAMARA	TAPA	TASMANIAN DEVIL
TAMARACK	TAP DANCE	TASMAN LIGHT
TAMARIND	TAPFER	TASTE OF HONEY
TAMARISK	TAPIOCA	TASTY LADY
TAMARLANE	TAPIR	TA TA
TAMBIEN	TAPPAHANNOCK	TATAMI
TAMBOR	TAPROOT	TATAR
TAMBORINE	TAPS	TATAU
TAMMY	TARA	TATER
TAMPA	TARANTULA	TA-TL
TAMPALPAIS	TARASHANTI	TATOOSH

TATTOO	TEASE	TELLY
T & T	TEASE ME	TELSTAR
TAURUS	TEASER	TEMA MAR
TAUTOG	TEA SPOON	TEMBLAR
TAWA	TECH	TEMPAS
TAWNY EAGLE	TECH DREAM	TEMPERANCE
TAX CUTTER	TECHNO LIFE	TEMPEST
TAXISTA	TECNICA	TEMPLE
T. BEAR	TECUMSEH	TEMPO
T BIRD	TEDDY	TEMPOS
TCHAIKOVSKY	TEDDY BARE	TEMPTATION
TE	TEDDY BEAR	TEMPTING LADY
TEABERRY	T EDGE	TEMPTING TIGRESS
TEA CEREMONY	TEDU	TEMPTRESS

Intentionally mis(s)pelling to create a desired effect is accepted practice in boat naming: ACKWITAL, AIRONAUTICAL, BAY GUL, BULLION, COC PIT, CONNFUSION, DAILY DOZE, DIPSEA, DISTRAKSHUN, EMTEE POKETS, EXZAGGERATED, FOTO FINISH, F-RIGHTNING, FUNOFIT, FUNFORALL, GLOGIRL, GOLD NUGGIT, GRAN-MUDDER, GROOSOME TOOSOME, HI DOLLER, INCONSPICKUOUS, KOASTIN, KUTEY, LEGISLATER, LUSHIOUS, KRAFTI, MERRYMENT, MINDSWEEPER, MONKEY BIZNEZZ, MUZIC IN MY EARS, MYSTIRIOUS, NEWSENCE, NO BULL, PROMOCEAN, RAZZ MA TAZZ, RHAPSADY, ROGUES GALLEY, ROTSA RUCK, RUMAWAY, SALTY DAWG, SEACLUSION, SEACLUSIVE, SEADUCER, SEAIRA, SEA NARIO, SHOGON, SINSATION, SKILFUL, SMALL WERL, SOO FAST, SPLASHDANCE, SUM TOY, TACKFUL, TINY TING, TOOO MUCH, TRANCE FER, TRIPTYCH, TUNSA FUN, TWO GRIT, UNORTHODOCKS, VEDDY NICE, VITAMIN SEA, WANDEROUS, X CALIBER, X-CITATION, X TERMINATOR, XTRA, and ZIN ZA SCHUN.

TEACHER	TEDUVE	TEMPUS
TEACHER'S PET	TEDUVERI	TEMPUS FUGIT
TEACHER'S PETTER	TEENIE BOPPER	TEN
TEACHING MACHINE	TEENY WEENIE	TEN +
TEA HOUSE	TEETER TOTTER	TENACIOUS
TEAL	TEETH	TENACITY
TEAM APACHE	TEE TIME	TENCENDUR
TEAM DREAM	TEETINA	TENCHI
TEAM GULFWIND	TEETOTALER	TENDER
TEAM SPORT	TEHINI	TENDER DANCER
TEAM _____	TEJAS	TENDERFOOT
TEARDROP	TELEPATHY	TENDER FLOWER
TEAR 'EM UP	TELESCOPE	TENDER MOTION
TEARS HAVE FALLEN	TELL NO ONE	TENDER POD

PLAYING WITH WORDS & LETTERS

TENDER TRAP
TENDER _____
_____ TENDER
TENDRIL
TE NEE
TENER DE TODO
TENER PRISA
TENER SUENO
TENGO TIEMPO
TE NI
TENJIN
TENNESSEE
TENNESSEE TEN
TENNYSON
TEN PLUS
TEN RUPEES
TENSION
TENSION AWAY

TERRAPIN
TERRIBLE
TERRIBLE TWOS
TERRIER
TERRIFIC
TESORO
TESSERACT
TESTEROSSA
TEST ME
TESTY ONE
TETE A TETE
TETON
TETRA
TEUER
TEUTONIC
TE VEGA
TEXAN
TEXAS

THAT'S MY HON
THAT _____
THE ARK
THE ATLAS
THE BATTLE OF NEW
  ORLEANS
THE BEST
THE BEST REVENGE
THE BETTER LIFE
THE BIG DAWG
THE BITTER END
THE BLUE GOOSE
THE BRIARPATCH
THE BUTLER DID IT
THE CANDYMAN
THE CATS MEOW
THE 'CISCO KID
THE DREAMER

Abbreviations are recognized by boaters as having a place in boat names. Individuals may modify the accepted meaning for their particular boats, but these reductions will be recognized anyway. Some unusual abbreviations include: A over T (British slang: asbestos over tea kettle; topsy-turvy, or, ass over tit), AWB (average white boat), AWOL (absent without leave), B&B, C.E.O., C.O.D., CO OP, DMZ, DNA, DOT, EHF, EKG, EZ, GHQ, HI FI, J.R., L*A*S*S, LIFO (last in, first out), M&M (candy), Nth,° NYSE, OK, OPM (other people's money), O.J.T., O.T., PDQ, PJ's, PNL (profit & loss), P.O.S.H., P.S., PTL, PTO, QC, QE II, R&R (rest and relaxation), RPM, TNT, TSOP (the sound of Philadelphia), UFO (unidentified flying object), "V," VC, and VIP.

TENSPEED
TENTATIVA
TENT MAKER
TEN YEARS AFTER
TEO
TEPEE
TEPIC
TEQUILA
TEQUILA 'N SALT
TEQUILA SUNRISE
TEQUILA SUNSET
TERAS
TERI
TERMINATOR
TERMITE'S DELIGHT
TERN
TERN TOO
TERRA NOVA

TEXAS BELL
TEXAS ROSE
TEXAS _____
TEX MEX
TEXTURES
THALAMUS
THAI STICK
THANKFUL
THANKS
THANKS DAD
THANX
THAT CAT
THAT FUNKY MUSIC
THAT NIGHT
THAT OLD BLACK
  MAGIC
THAT'S ANUFF
THAT'S LIFE

THE EDGE
THE ELIZABETH
THEE 'N ME
THE FAR SIDE
THE GIFT
THE GRAPEVINE
THE GREAT
  PRETENDER
THEIRS
THE KID
THE LAST PHOTON
THELMA
THE LOCO-MOTION
THE LONE RANGER
THE MAGIC DRAGON
THE MAGICIAN
THE MAIN EVENT
THE MALLARD

THE MEN'S CLUB
THEME SONG
THE MIDNIGHT HOUR
THE MOST
THE MOST BEAUTIFUL
  GIRL
THE OFFICE
THEOS
THE OSPREY
THE OTHER BITCH
THE PURPLE PEOPLE
  EATER
THERA P.
THERAPUTIC
THERAPY
THEREAFTER
THE RED BARON
THERESA
THERMOPYLAE

THE WORLD
THIMBLE
THINES MINE
THING
_____ THING
THINK AGAIN
THINKER
THIRD DEGREE
THIRD DIMENSION
THIRD EYE
THIRD SON
THIRD WORLD
THIS BE IT
THIS IS IT
THIS TIME
THISTLE
THLALOCA
THOMAS JEFFERSON
THON

THREE WISHES
THRENODY
THRESHER
THRILLER
THROTTLE RESPONSE
THROWBACK
THRUSH
THUMPER
THUNDER
THUNDERBIRD
THUNDERBOLT
THUNDER BOLT
THUNDER CLAP
THUNDER CLOUD
THUNDER DANCER
THUNDERDUST
THUNDERER
THUNDER HUNTER
THUNDER STRUCK

With boat names, abbreviations can be defined as you choose. Some more are: ABC, CSA, D.A.V., ERA, F.O.B., IOOF, LOOM, NSW, QED, RSVP, S BY SE, and a dinghy: P.S.

Onomatopoeia, the creation of words depicting familiar sounds, can be very effective: Awwwwww, BLAM, B'RRR, Bzzzzzz, Grrrrrr or GRRR, HA HA HA, MMMM, MMMMMMM, OH-OH, OOMPAPA, OOO-LA-LA, Ooooh, OOOO-WEEEE, OOO WEE, PITTER PATTER, POOH, RAZZMATAZZ, RING A DING, UH HUH, UH OH!, U LA LA, VA-ROOM, WHAM BAM, WHIZ BANG, WOO HA, and ZZZ, and ZZZIP.

THERMOS
THE SAMURAI
THESE DREAMS
THESEUS
THE SEVEN C'S
THE SHADOW
THESIS
THE SOURCE
THE SPIRIT
THE SPIRIT OF _____
THESPIS
THE SPRUCE GOOSE
THE STAR
THE STRIPPER
THETA
THETIS
THE TURTLE
THE WANDERER
THE WANTON

THORA
THOREAU
THORIN
THORN BIRD
THORNY DEVIL
THORO LEE GOOD
THOROUGHBRED
THOR'S GIRL
THOR'S HAMMER
THRASHER
THREADFIN
THREE BELLES
THREE BELLS
THREE CHEERS
THREE FOXES
THREE GENERATIONS
THREE SISTERS
THREE STARS
THREE TIMES A LADY

THURSDAY'S CHILD
THYME
TI
TIA
TIA JUANA
TIAMA
TIA MARIA
TIANA
TI AMOR
TIARA
TIARE
TIARE TAHITI
TIBURON
TICKET A LEAVE
TICKET TO RIDE
TICKLE ME QUICKLY
TICKLER
TICKLER FRANCIE
TICKLISH

17

Bon Voyage:

Other Language Sources & Jargon

Names influenced by the American Indian include: BUCK WELL SPENT, CHIEF, CHIEFTAN, COCHISE, COMANCHE, CRAZY HORSE, KICKPOO, LONE EAGLE, LONE WOLF, MEDICINE MAN, MEDICINE WOMAN, MOHAWK, MOHICAN, MORNING CLOUD, NAVAJO, ONONDAGA, PAPOOSE, PALEFACE, PEACE PIPE, POCAHONTAS, POW WOW, RAINDANCE, RUNNING BEAR, SAVAGE WARRIOR, SAVY, SCALPER, SEMINOLE, SHAWNEE, SHOOTING STAR, SIOUX, SISSETON, SPOTTED HORN, TENDERFOOT, TEPEE, TONTO, TOMAHAWK, WACCAMAW, WAR DANCE, and WINNEBAGO.

TICONDEROGA	TIGER MOTH	TIME & SPACE
TIC TAK TOE	TIGER PAWS	TIME AWAY
TIC TOK	TIGER RAG	TIME BANDIT
TIDAL WAVE	TIGER'S EYE	TIME IN A BOTTLE
TIDA WAVE	TIGER'S HEART	TIMELESS
TIDBIT	TIGER'S PAW	TIMELESS FLIGHT
TIDE	TIGHT 'N FINE	TIMELY
TIDELINE	TIGHTROPE	TIME MACHINE
TIDES	TIGHTWAD	TIME OFF
TI DI	TIGRESS	TIME OUT
TIED ONE ON	TIKI	TIMES EXPRESS
TIEMPO	TILA	TIME SPLENDOR
TIENTOS	TILIKUM	TIME TAGO
TIFFANY GIRL	TIL MANANA	TIME WARP
TIGER	TIMBERWIND	TIMEWINDS
TIGERESS	TIMBER WOLF	TIME ZONE
TIGER HEAT	TIMBRE	TIME _____
TIGER INSTINCTS	TIMBUK II	_____ TIME
TIGER LILLY	TIME AFTER TIME	TIMPANI

TIM TAM	TITANIUM	TONAL
TINA	TITUS	TONALA
TINA MARIE	TIVAKA	TONI
TINAVETTE	TIVKA	TONIC
TIN CAN	TIVOLI	TONIGHT'S STAR
TINE	TIZY	TONTO
TINEY HINEY	TIZZI	TONYA
TINKER	TIZZY	TOO
TINKERBELLE	T.L.C.	TOODLE TIME
TINKER TOY	T N A	TOOK A CHANCE
TIN MAN	T N T	TOOK ME AWAY
TINORS	TOBAGO	TOO MUCH
TINSEL	TO BE SURE	TOOO MUCH
TINY BUBBLE	TOCAR MI TIMBRE	TOO QUICK
TINY PAWS	TODDLER	TOOTH 'N NAIL
TINY TING	TO DO	TOOTH FAIRY
TINY TUSH	TOE TAPPER	_____ TOO
TIPI	TO EXCESS	TOPAZ

Language translation guides or handbooks used for foreign travel will often lead to unique and pleasing name choices. Since most of the English language is derived from other linguistic sources, particularly American English, we have included a sampling of both actual and potential names.

If possible, avoid names having an unexpected meaning in a foreign language, especially if you plan to visit an area using that language: While the French À LA MODE (current, fashionable, prevailing, up-to-date), or À LA KING (fit for a king) is nice anywhere. À LA CARTE (on the card), or MAL DE MER (sea-sickness), may sound curious in some quarters.

TIP OFF	TOGETHER	TOP 40 (20, 30, ETC)
TIPPACANOE	TOGETHER AT LAST	TOP BRASS
TIPPY CANOE	TOGWOTEE	TOP CAT
TIPSTER	TOKEM	TOPCAT
TIPSY	TOKYO MAID	TOP ECHELON
TIPSY DOODLE	TOKYO TANGO	TOP GUN
TIPSY TOO	TOLSTOY	TOPIC
TIPTOE	TOLTEC	TOP HAT 'N TAILS
TIP TOP	TOMAHAWK	TOP KNOT
TIRED	TOM BOY	TOPLESS DANCER
TIRED O' TOIL	TOM CAT	TOP LINE
TIRELESS	TOM CATTEN	TOPPER
TIROL	TOM DOOLEY	TOPPLER
TISKET A TASKET	TOMFOOLERY	TOPPY
TITA	TOMIC	TOPSY
TITAN	TOMKAT	TOP SECRET
TITANIA	TOM THUMB	TOPSY
TITANIC	TOMTIT	TOP _____

TORCH
TOREADOR
TORII
TORMENTA
TORMENTOR
TORN
TORNADO
TORONADO
TORPEDO
TORQUED
TORREY CANYON

TOUCHA CLASS
TOUCHDOWN
TOUCHÉ
TOUCH O' CLASS
TOUCH OF CLASS
TOUCHY SUBJECT
TOUGH TIMES
TOUGH WARRIOR
TOUJOURS
TOUPEE
TOUR DE FORCE

TRACE TRACKER
TRACHEA
TRACKLESS
TRACKS
TRADEWIND
TRAFTNUC
TRAILBLAZER
TRAIL SEEKER
TRAILS END
TRAMP
TRAMP TIME

BASNIGHT

TORTOISE
TORTOLA
TORTUGA
TOSCANA
TOSCIN
TOSSIN' AND TURNIN'
TOSTEN COFFEE
TOTEM
TOTO
TOUCAN
TOUCH A CLASS

TOUR GUIDE
TOUROMANIA
TOWBAAVANI
TO WIN
TOWN'S END
TOY
TOY GEORGE
TOY TOY
TOZAN
TRACER
TRACE TREKKER

TRANCE
TRANCE CONDUCTOR
TRANCE FER
TRANCE INDUCER
TRANQUILITY
TRANQUILIZER
TRANQUILO
TRANQUIL CANOE
TRANQUIL EYES
TRANQUIL REALMS
TRANQUIL ROAMER

TRANSCENDENCE	TRELLIS	TRIPLE DEE
TRANSCENDENT	TREMOLO	TRIPLE FANTASY
TRANSFIXED	TREND SETTER	TRIPLE PLAY
TRANSFORM	TRENDY	TRIPLE SEC
TRANSFORMATIONAL	TREPIDATION	TRIPLE THREAT
TRANSIENT	TRES EN TRES	TRIPLE TROUBLE
TRANSIT	TRES JIF	TRIPOLI
TRANSITADO	TREU	TRIPPER
TRANSITION	TRIAD	TRIPTYCH
TRANS OCEANIC	TRIAL	TRISHEN
TRANSPLANTER	TRIAL TACTICS	TRISTAN
TRANSVERSE	TRIBAL HUNTER	TRISTAR
TRANS_____	TRIBE RANGER	TRI-STAR
TRATAR	TRICE	TRITON
TRAUMA	TRICERION	TRI TONE
TRAVACREST SEAWAY	TRICIA	TRI UMPH

The French language provides many romantic names, many of which may be familiar: A'COMPTE (on account), AVOCAT (lawyer), BEAUS YEUS (good looks), CHERE AMIE (dear female friend), CONFRERE (colleague), DISTINGUÉ (elegant appearance), ELANCER (to dart), EN ROUTE (on the way), ÉLITE (the best), FLEUR (flower), MA CHERE (my dear), MON AMI (my friend), NOBLESSE OBLIGE (obligation to behave nobly or kindly), OISEAU DE FEU (firebird), PENCHER (assumed), QUAND MÊME (whatever may), QUI VA LÀ (who goes there?), QUI VIVE (challenge), RACONTEUR (teller of stories), RAISON D'ÊTRE (reason for existance), RÉNÈGARE (to deny), REVEILLEZ (awaken), SAUMON (salmon), SAVOIR-VIVRE (good breeding), SOI-DISTANT (self-styled), TARGE (shield), THON (tuna), VENIR (come), VIS À VIS (face to face), VIVA LA BAGATELLEL (long live frivolity), VOILÀ TOUT (that's all), and VOLER (to fly).

TRAVAIL	TRICKSTER	TRIUMPH
TRAVEL AGENT	TRIDENT	TRO FEE
TRAVELER	TRIED 'N TRUE	TROFEO
_____TRAVELER	TRIGGER	TROIKA
TRAVELLER'S JOY	TRIGGERFISH	TROJAN HORSE
TRAVELING CIRCUS	TRIGUENA	TROLL
TRAVELIN' MAN	TRIK R TREAT	TROLLOP
TRAVESTEVERE	TRILLIUM	TRONAR
TRAX	TRIMESTER	TROON
TREASURE	TRIMURTI	TROOPER
TREASURED TIME	TRINE	TROPHY
TREASURE HUNTER	TRINITY	TROPHY BOX
TREE FORMER	TRINKET	TROPICALE
TREE FROG	TRIO	TROPICAL TRADER
TREKKA	TRIO O' DAZZLERS	TROPICAL TREADER
TREIBHOLZ	TRIPLE CROWN	TROPICAT

TROPIC BIRD	TUFF ENUFF	TWIDDLE DEE
TROPIC LIGHTNING	TUFFY	TWITTLE DUM
TROPI_____	TUMBLEWEED	TWIGGY
TROTTER	TUMERIC	TWILIGHT MOODS
TROUBADOUR	TUNA MARINE	TWILIGHT RUN
TROUBLE MAKER	TUNA TANGO	TWILIGHT SONGS
TROUBLEMAKER	TUNED IN	TWILIGHT TIME
TROUBLE SEEKER	TUNEFUL	TWILIGHT ZONE
TROUBLE SHOOTER	TUNG	TWILIGHT _____
TROUNCER	TUNGSTEN	TWIN BILL
TROUSSE	TUNING FORK	TWINKLE TOES
TROUT	TUNIS	TWIRLER
TROY WEIGHT	TUNSA FUN	TWISTED SISTER
TRUANT	TUNU	TWISTED SISTERS
TRUDY	TUN WU	TWISTER
TRUE BLUE	TURBO LOVER	TWISTY
TRUE LOVE	TURBOT	TWISTY BRITCHES
TRUELOVE	TURISTA	TWITORIAL
TRUE LUFF	TURK	TWO B SURE
TRUE LUST	TURMOIL	TWO CAN

Examples of Hawaiian boat names include: AKAMAI (wise), AKEAKAMAI (lover of wisdom), ALII (royalty), ALOHA (love, kindness, affection, good will; greeting or farewell), AMAAMA (mullet), KALA (unicorn fish), KAPU (keep out, taboo), KA'U (a District in Hawaii), HALE (house), HALE KAI (sea house), HANUI (parrot fish), HAPUUPUU (grouper), IOLANI (queen), IO NEST (hawk's nest), KAHAK∴ (amberjack), KAILANI (heavenly seas), KANE (Chief God, man), KAPU (keep out, taboo), KEALAKEKUA (way of the God), KOLE (surgeon fish), KU (God of War), KUMU (red goat fish), LANI (sky), LIMU (seaweed), MALIHINI (newcomer), and MANU KAI (sea bird).

TRUE MOTION	TURNED ON	TWO DOGS 'N A CAT
TRUE NORTH	TURNING POINT	TWO FOLD
TRUE RUN	TURN ON	TWO GRIT
TRUE TEMPER	TURQUOISE	TWO IF BY SEA
TRUE TO YOU	TURTLE	TWO KEELED
TRUE _____	TURTLE DOVE	TWO MORROW
TRULY FAIR	TUSCANY	TWO'S A CROWD
TRUMP CARD	TUTELAGE	TWOSOME
TRUMPETER SWAN	TUTI FRUTI	TWO STARS
TRU PERFORMER	TUTTI FRUTTI	TWO STEP
TRUST FUND	TUTU	TWOSTEP
TRUSTY STAR	TUXEDO NIGHTS	TWO TIMER
TRYST	TWAIN MET	TWO TRIBES
T.S.O.P.	TWANGIEST	_____ TWO
TSUNAMI	TWEED	TYCOON
TUB	TWEEK ME	TYGER
TUCKERED OUT	TWEETIE BIRD	TYMPANUM
TUDOR	TWEEZER	TYPE A
TUESDAY'S CHILD	TWENTY-FOUR KARAT	TYPE B
TUFF ACT	TWICE AS NICE	TYPEE

TYPHOON
TYPHOON TOMMY
TYRO
TZU
TZU HANG

U

U F O
UGLY DUCKLING
UH OH!
UH-OH
UIGHER
UKIAH

UNCKA
UNCLE
UNCOUTH
UNCROWDED SEAS
UNCTION
UNDAUNTED
UNDERGROUND
 ECONOMY
UNDER THUMB
UNDER WAY
UNDERWAY
UNDINE
UND SO WEITER
UNDULATE
UNDULATOR
UNH HUH
UNIALGAL

UNSURPASSED
UNSWERVING
UNTAINTED
UNTENABLE
UNTIRING
UNWINDER
UPBEAT
UPLIFTER
UPPER CLASS
UPPER CRUST
UPROAR
UPROARIOUS
UPSHOT
UPSTART
UPTEMPO
UPTOWN
UPTOWN GIRL

More Hawaiian names are: MOMI (pearl), OPAKAPAKA (pink snapper), PANIOLO (cowboy), PAU HANA (finished work), PAULANI (heaven's end), PIKAKE (jasmine), POOU (wrasse), PUA KAI (sea flower), PUKI (eel), PUPU (tidbits), TATAU (tattoo), TITA (tomboy), UHU (parrotfish), UKU (snapperfish), ULUA (jackfish), and WEKE (goatfish).

In popular "pidgin": BAMBUCHA (big), COASTING (unemployed, not busy), GOOD FUN (better than just fun), HANA HOU (do it one more time), HUMBUG (bother, hassle), MO'BETTAH (better), OKOLE (buttocks, hiney), ONREAL (unreal), SHAKA (right on!), S'KOSHI (little bit), SUCK WIND (get lost), TO DA MAX (all the way), WE GO (let's split), WHATEVAHS (whatever), and WODDASCOOPS (what's happening?).

UKULELE
ULTIMATE
ULTIMATE HIGH
ULTIMATE _____
ULTRAHIGH
ULTRAINDESTRUCT-
ULTRA SEA   IBLE
ULYSSES
UMBILICAL CORD
UMBRELLA
UMIAK
UMPIRE
UNBEATEN
UNBOUND
UNBRIDLED
UNCHAINED
UNCHAINED MELODY
UNCIVIL

UNICORN
UNION
UNIQUE ASSEMBLAGE
UNISON
UNISTAR
UNIVERSAL
UNIVERSITY
UNKNOWN SAILOR
U NO
UNO
UNORTHODOX
UNORTHODOCKS
UNPARALLED
UNPOLITICAL
UNPRECEDENTED
UNRIVALLED
UNSHAKEN
UNSPARING

UPWARD
UP YOURS
UPYORS
URSUS
USED
USE ME
USHUAIA
US UN'S
UTAH
UTMOST
UTOPIA

V

VAADA JEHANI
VAARUTA

OTHER LANGUAGE SOURCES & JARGON

VAAVU	VALIGIA	VARA RITI
VA BIDI	VALIUM	VARA UFAA
VACATE	VALKYRIE	VA RANGALU
VACILLATOR	VALLEY GIRL	VARIABLE STYLE
VAE VICTUS	VALLURE	VARIVE
VAGA	VALMOUR	VARMIT CHASER
VAGABOND	VALORFUL	VARNISH
VAGABONDAGE	VAL'S BABE	VA-ROOM
VAGABUNDO	VALU BULL	VASA
VAGARIOUS	VALUE	VASHTI
VAGARI	VALUED	VAST NESS
VAGATU	VAMOS	VAST SHORES
VAGRANT	VAMOOSE	VATE AHEAD
VAHAKA	VAMPS VUFOONERY	VATES
VAHINE	VANDAL	VAUDEVILLE
VAHALLA	VANADIS	VA VOOOM
VAHEVALA	VANANI	V C

*Japanese boat names add intriguing expression: **DAINICHITER** (god of the sun), **GIRI** (duty), **IN ITICHINEN** (life-essence), **INKA** (seal of approval), **JAHO** (magic), **JITSU** (fullness), **JIT SURYOKU** (superhuman powers), **JUNSUISEI** (purity of resolve), **KENDO** (swordsmanship), **KIMI** (friend), **KU** (god of war), **KYOKI** (madness), **MAHO-ZUKAI** (sorcerer), **MICHI** (the unknown path), **MIKO** (sorceress), **MONDO** (question and answer), **MYOKO** (fine luster), **OBA-CHAMA** (grandmother), **OGI** (fan), **OHKA** (cherry blossom), **ONSHITSU** (arrogance), **RENGE** (lotus flower), **RINKIOHEN** (adaptability to all circumstances), **RYOKAN** (Zen monk/poet), **SABI** (lonliness), **SHIKAN MAKA** (vast ocean), **SHO** (birth), **SHOMON** (state of learning), **SHUJO SHO YURAKU** (happiness in this life), **SONO-MAMA** (just so), **SUNYA** (void), **TANDEN** (inner strength), **TOZAN** (head temple), and **YUJUTSU** (water, spring).*

VAIL	VANDYKE	VEDA
VAIN	VANESSA	VEDDY NICE
VAINA	VANGUARD	VEE
VAKASHUN	VAN GO	VEEP
VAKEELU	VAN GOGH	VEE SEA
VALCOCEUR	VANGUARD	VEETE AHEAD
VALHALLA	VANILLA	VEGA
VALE	VANITY	VELAA
VALENCIA	VANNA	VELAZQUEZ
VALENTINE	VANQUISHED	VELELLA
VALERE	VANQUISHER	VELHO
VALERO	VAN TASTIC	VELOCITY
VALERY	VAPOR	VELOX
VALET	VAPORIZER	VELVET FINISHER
VALI	VARA BARA	VELVET INTERLUDE
VALIANT	VARA GADA	VEME A MI
VALID LADY	VARA MIRU	VENCER

VENDETTA
VEN DOOR
VENERABLE
VENEZIA
VENG
VENGEANCE
VENIR
VENI VIDI VICI
VENOMOUS
VENTANA

VERBATIM
VERDAD
VERBENA
VERBUM
VERBUM SAT SAPIENTI
VERDI
VERDICT
VERI HAPPI
VERITY
VERMILLION

VERSEATILE
VERSED 'N WIND
VERTEX
VERTIGO
VERTUE
VERTWO
VERUS
VERVE
VERY LEE
VERY MUCH

VENTED WRATH
VENTURA
VENTURE
VENTURE FORTH
VENTURER
VENTURESOME
VENTURI EFFECT
VENUS
VERACRUZ
VERANO

VERMILLION
  WARRIOR
VERMOUTH
VERNAL
VERNONIX
VERONICA
VERONIER
VERRAZANO
VERSAILLES
VERSARI

VERY NICE
VES
VESPERS
VESPER SPARROW
VESPUCCI
VESTA
VESTAL
VESUVIUS
VETERE
VETTE

OTHER LANGUAGE SOURCES & JARGON

VEXARE
VIA
VIA JERO
VIAJERO
VIBES
VIBRAHARP
VIBRANCE
VIBRANT CHILD
VIBRANT DRUMS
VIBRAPHONE
VIBRATO
VIBRATOR
VIBRO
VICE
VICE'S NICE
VICE'S REWARDS

VIDA
VIDA VIDA
VIDDLES
VIDEO
VIDYA
VIENNA
VIENTO
VIERA
VIGIL
VIGILANCE
VIGILANT
VIGOROUS
VIHA
VIHI
VIKARA
VIKI

VINYL DOLL
VIOLET
VIOLET VISION
VIOLIN
V I P
VIPER
VIPER FISH
VIREO
VIRGA
VIRGEN
VIRGIL
VIRGINIA
VIRGINIA
   GENTLEMAN
VIRGINIA REEL
VIRGINIA _____

---

*Latin continues in popular phrases recognized as boat names: **ALTER EGO** (counterpart, double), **ARCADES AMBO** (two rascals), **MAGNUM BONUM** (a great good, a boon), **MODUS OPERANDI** (manner of working), **FIDUS ACHATES** (a true friend), **QUID PRO QUO** (something for something), **SALIRE** (to leap), **SILVA** (forest, wood), **TEMPUS** (time), **UBIQUE** (everywhere), **ULTER** (beyond), **ULULARE** (howl), **UMBRA** (shade), **UNUS** (one), **VAGARI** (wander), **VALE** (farewell), **VALERE** (be strong), **VATES** (prophet), **VELOX** (swift), **VENI VIDI VICI** (I came, I saw, I conquered), **VERUS** (true), **VETERE** (to turn), **VERSARI** (be busy), **VEXARE** (agitate), **VICIS** (change), **VIDEO** (I see), **VINCERE** (to conquer), **VIRGINIBUS PUERISQUE** (for maidens and boys), **VIS A TERGO** (a force from behind), **VIS VITAE** (force of life), **VITIUM** (vice), **VOLUPTAS** (pleasure), **VORARE** (devour), **VOTUM** (solemn promise), and **VULPIS** (fox).*

VICE VERSA
_____'S VICE
VICI
VICIS
VICTIM
VICTOR
VICTOREE
VICTORIA
VICTORIOUS
VICTORIOUS WENCH
VICTORY
VIC TORY
VICTORY LANE
VICTRESS
VICTRIDE
VICUNA

VIKING
VILLA
VILLAGE A SEA
VIM 'N VIGOR
VIMPIE
VINCERE
VINCI
VINDICATOR
VINDICTA
VINDU
VINDY SEA
VINE FLYER
VINEYARD MORNING
VINISHED
VINNIE
VINTAGE

VIRGINIBUS
   PUERISQUE
VIRGIN SLUT
VIRGO
VIRGO LADY
VIRTUD
VIRTUE
VIRULENT
VISAARE
VIS A TERGO
VIS A VIS
VISION QUEST
VISNANI
VISSARE DUNI
VISCOUNT
VISCOUNTESS

VISHNU
VISION
VISIONARY
VISION SEEKER
VISITA
VISNUNG GADA
VISTA MAR
VISUAL MEDIUM
VIS VITE
VITA
VITALITY
VITAL LUST
VITAMIN SEA
VITESSE
VITIUM
VITRO
VITULUS
VIVA!

VOLADOR
VOLAR
VOLATILE
VOLCANIC
VOLER
VOLPLANE
VOLSTEAD ACT
VOLTAGE METER
VOLTAIRE
VOLTAIC GIRL
VOLTARE
VOLTS A WIND
VOLUNTARY EXILE
VOLUNTEER
VOLUPTAS
VOLUPTUARY
VOLVER LOCO
VOLVERSE LOCO

VULCANIZER
VULGER SON
VULPINE
VULPINE VIXEN
VULPES
VULTURE

W

WABASH
WABASH CANNONBALL
WABE
WACCAMAW
WACHOLDER

German names include: *GEMÜTLICH (cozy), LAGUNE FRAULEIN (lagoon girl), LANZE (spear, lance), LECHZEN MEER (yearn for the ocean), LEITER (leader), LIBELLE (dragonfly), LIEBLING (favorite), LIEBCHEN (girlfriend-lover), LILLIE (lilly), LUFTCHEN (gentle breeze), LYRISCH (lyrical), NACHBIS (see you later), NACHSOMMER (Indian summer), NICKERCHEN (forty winks), NIXIE (mermaid), QUAKEN (duck), QUALEN (tormentor), QUASTE (powder puff), QUATSCH (nonsense), QUELLE (spring, fountain), RABE (raven), RACHE (vengeance), RAKETE (rocket), RASSE (race), SAGENHAFT (legendary), SAHNE (cream), SALDIEREN (balance), SAMT (velvet), SCHARFE (sharp), SCHATZ (darling, sweetheart), SCHEU (shy), and SCHNABEL (beak of a bird of prey).*

VIVACIOUS
VIVACE
VIVA LA BAGATELLEL
VIVA LOLITA
VIVANT
VIVE LA LIBERTE
VIVRE
VIXEN
VIXO
VIXON
VIZ
VIZOR
VLAD TEPES
VOCIFEROUS
VOGUE ROGUE
VOICE OVER
VOILA TOUT
VOL AU VENT

VOODOO
VOODOO MAGIC
VOODOO VAMP
VOO DOO BABY
VOO DOO CHILD
VORACIOUS
VORARE
VORTEX VANDA
VOTARY
VOTUM
VOUCHER
VOW 'N VOTIVE
VOYAGE A ZEN
VOYAGER
VOYAGEUR
VOYEUR
VU FINDER
VULCAN

WACHLUND
WACHSAM
WACHTEL
WACHTER
WACKER
WACKY
WAD'A BUCKS
WADER
WAFF
WAG
WAGE ERN R
WAGEMUT
WAGEN
WAGNER
WAG TAIL
WAGTAIL
WAHCONDA
WAHINE

OTHER LANGUAGE SOURCES & JARGON

WAHNSINN
WAHOO
WAHREN
WAIF
WAIMEA
WAINBOW
WAITING GAME
WAIT NOT
WAIT NOT WANT NOT
WAKAN TANKA
WAKE
WAKEA
WAKEFUL
WAKE UP
WAL
WALDEN
WALE RISER

WANDERLUST
WANGKA
WANKEL
WANT TO
WANTON
WANTON WAIF
WANT TOO
WAPITI
WAPPENKUNDE
WAR BABY
WARBLER
WAR CHIEF
WAR EAGLE
WARI·
WARLOCK
WARLORD
WARM RAIN

WASHINGTON
WASP
WASSAIL
WATCH DOG
WATCH OUT
WATCH WORD
WATERBEARER
WATER BED
WATERBED
WATER CHESTNUT
WATERCOCK
WATERCOLOR
WATER COOLER
WATER DANCER
WATER FEVER
WATER FIX
WATER FLIGHTS

*More German names: **SCHNELL** (swift, fast), **SEGLER** (fast sailor), **SEHER** (seer, prophet), **ÜBERFALL** (surprise), **ÜBERMUTIG** (frolicsome), **ULK** (joker), **UMFAHREN** (sail around), **UNART** (naughty), **UNGEDULD** (impatient), **UNSCHULD** (innocent), **UHU** (eagle, owl), **UND SO WEITER** (and so forth), **URLAUB** (holiday), **WABE** (honeycomb), **WACHOLDER** (juniper), **WACHSAM** (vigilant), **WACHTEL** (quail), and **WACHTER** (guardian), **WACKER** (gallant), **WAGEMUT** (daring), **WAGEN** (venture), **WAHNSINN** (insanity), **WAL** (whale), **WALZER** (waltz), **WANDERJAHR** (year of wander), **WAPPENKUNDE** (heraldry), **WARUM** (why), **WEGRAND** (wayside), **WEGWEISER** (guide), **WEIB** (wife), **WEIBERHELD** (ladies man), **WESPE** (wasp), **WIEDER** (again), **WIEHERN** (neigh), **WILDE** (wild), and **WINDROSE** (compass card).*

WALKING STICK
WALKING TALL
WALLEYE
WALLFLOWER
WALLON
WALLOPER
WALL STREET
WALRUS
WALTZ
WALZER
WAM PUM
WAN AWAY
WAND
WANDER BIRD
WANDERER
WANDERING JEW
WANDERJAHR

WAR DANCE
WAR HORSE
WAR LORD
WARLORD
WAR PAINT
WARPATH
WAR PONY
WARP SPEED
WARREN
WARRIOR
WARRIOR'S RIDE
WARRIOR'S PONY
WART HOG
WARUM
WAR WHOOP
WARZE
WASHAKIE

WATERFOWL
WATER GAME
WATER IMAGE
WATERLAND
WATER LILLY
WATERLOO
WATER LOVE
WATERMAN
WATER MANTRA
WATER MOCCASIN
WATER MUSIC
WATERPROOF
WATER RAT
WATER REALM
WATER SHADOWS
WATERSHIP UP
WATER SOLO

WATER SONGS	WAY TO GO	WELCOME
WATER SPIRIT	WAYWARD	WELFARE
WATER SPOUT	WAYWARD SON	WELKIN
WATER TAPESTRY	WAYWARD LADY	WELL BEHAVED
WATER VALET	WAYWEGO	WELL BRED
WATER VOICE	WE	WELL DESERVED
WATER WAY	WEAPON	WELL HEELED
WATERWAY	WEASEL	WELL NIGH
WATER WEAVER	WEATHERBEE	WELL TO DO
WATER WINDOW	WEB	WELL TURNED
WATER WINGS	WEB FOOTED	WENCH
WATER WOMAN	WEB WE WEAVE	WELL WISHER
WATER WOOLF	WEDDED	WELSH PRINCESS
WATERWORKS	WEDDING BAND	WELT
WATER WORLD	WEDLOCK	WENAN
WATER _____	WEE	WENCEL
WAVE BABY	WEED	WENDY
WAVE DANCER	WEEKEND WARRIOR	WENDY 'N PETER

---

*Still more German names are: **WINSELN** (whimper), **WIPPE** (seesaw), **WURF** (cast), **WEISUNG** (directive), **WELT** (world), **WOLKEN BRUCH** (cloudburst), **WOLLUST** (voluptuousness), **WONNIG** (delight, blissful), **WÜHLER** (agitator), **WUNDER** (wonder), **WURDE** (dignity), **WUT** (rage, fury), **XMAL** (many times), **ZANKISCH** (quarrelsome), **ZART MADCHEN** (gentle girl), **ZARTLICH** (loving), **ZAUBER** (enchantment), **ZAUBERIN** (sorceress), **ZEICHEN** (sign), **ZEITGEIST** (time-spirit), **ZEITLEBENS** (for life), **ZERRBILD** (caricature), **ZU** (to), **ZUCHTHENGST** (stallion), **ZUGABE** (encore), **ZÜGELLOS** (unbridled), **ZUGLEICH** (together), **ZUGVOGEL** (migrating bird), **ZÜNDEN** (arouser), **ZUVIEL** (one too many), **ZUCHTIG** (chaste), **ZWECK** (purpose), **ZWILLING** (twins), **ZWINKERN** (wink), and **ZYNIKER** (cynic).*

WAVE CHISEL	WEE LUFF	WENCH
WAVE GLOW	WEE NEE ROSE	WENT
WAVE KING	WEE PISKEY	WERONIKA
WAVELENGTH	WEE SOLUTION	WERR THEE
WAVE MONARCH	WEE WENCH	WESGIN
WAVE QUEEN	WEE _____	WESPE
WAVEWALKER	WEGANDER	WESTERLY
WAVE WEAVER	WEGON	WESTERN GIRL
WAVE WHOOPIE	WEGRAND	WESTIN
WAVE WULF	WEGWEISER	WEST RUNNER
WAVE _____	WEHR	WEST VIRGINIA
WAVEY GRAVY	WEIB	WESTWARD HO
WA WA	WEIBERHELD	WET BACK
WAXWING	WEIDE	WET DREAM
WAYA	WEIGHTLESS	WE THREE
WAYFARER	WEIRDO	WET LOOK
WAYOUT	WEISUNG	WET 'N WILD
WAYOUT GIRL	WEKE	WET RIDER

WET WILLIE
WE TWO
WHACKER
WHALESONG
WHAM BAM
WHARF RAT
WHARF WENCH
WHAT
WHAT A FEELING
WHAT A GAS
WHAT A PACKAGE

WHIMSICAL LASS
WHIMSICAL MISS
WHIMSY
WHINNY
WHIP-IT
WHIPPER SNAPPER
WHIPPET
WHIP POOR WILL
WHIRLED ECSTASY
WHIRLER
WHIRLIGIG

WHITE
WHITE ARROW
WHITE BEARD
WHITE BOAT
WHITE BOWS
WHITECAP
WHITECAPS
WHITE CLOUD
WHITE COMET
WHITE CRUSADER
WHITE EAGLE

WHAT MAY
WHAT'S NEX
WHAT'S SHAKIN
WHEELER DEALER
WHELP
WHENEVER
WHET ME
WHIFF
WHIM
WHIMBREL
WHIMPER
WHIMSICAL JOURNEY

WHIRLING DERVISH
WHIRLWIND
WHIRLY GIRL
WHIRRING WHIFF
WHISKED AWAY
WHISKERS
WHISP
WHISPER
WHISTLE
WHISTLER
WHISTLER'S CHILD
WHISTLING DIXIE

WHITE FILLY
WHITEFIN
WHITEFISH
WHITE FOX
WHITE GIRL
WHITE GOLD
WHITE HAWK
WHITEHAWK
WHITE HEATHER
WHITE HUNTER
WHITE KNUCKLES
WHITE LIGHTNING

WHITE OUT	WHY KNOT	WILDCAT
WHITE RABBIT	WHY NOT	WILD CATTLE
WHITE RACE	WICCE	WILD CHERRY
WHITE ROSE	WICKED	WILD CHILD
WHITE SATIN	WICKED WANDA	WILD DUCK
WHITE SEAL	WICKER	WILDE
WHITE SLAVE	WIDE AWAKE	WILD EYED
WHITE SPORT COAT	WIDE VU	WILDFIRE
WHITE SUGAR	WIDE WY WORL	WILD FLOWER
WHITE TAIL	WIDGEON	WILD FOUL
WHITE TERN	WIDGET	WILD FOX
WHITE TIGER	WIDOW MAKER	WILD GOOSE
WHITE TRASH	WIEDER	WILD HARE
WHITE WARRIOR	WIEHERN	WILD HAIR
WHITE WINDS	WIELD R	WILD HORSE
WHITE WITCH	WIENER	WILDING
WHITHERER	WIFE 'N KIDS	WILD KAT

Maldivian: ALUVA (wind slave), ARRAM (leisure), ASDUNI (duck), AVAS (hurry), BARA (fast), BEFALU (noble class), BODU DUNI (big bird), BOLI (shell), BORVA (octopus), BULAA (cat), DARIEALU (offspring), DATURI, (voyage), DONKAMANA (white woman), DUVANI (to sail), ENDERI (black coral), FADIGN MAKUNU (spider), FAI (leaf), FATIHU (dawn), FUENBARI (Nautilus shell), FUHIVE (lonely), FUPA HANG (balloon), HAKEEM (medicine man), HANDU (moon), HENI (laugh), IHI (lobster), IRU (son), JAADU (magic), KARAA (melon), KORKA (butterfly), KORMAS (dolphin), KUDA BOLI (cowrie), KULI (spicy), KURUMBA (young coconut, LORBI (love), LORFINDU (dragonfly), MAS (fish), MOIA (mad), NASHANI (to dance), NASIBU (lucky), RAANI (queen), REETI (beautiful), RIA (sail), RITI (pretty), SABABU (reason), SABNAM (dew), SAFAI (tea leaves), and SAKARAI (ridiculous).

WHITISH	WIGEON	WILDLY FLYER
WHITMAN	WIGGED OUT	WILDLY FOE
WHITNEY	WIGGLE INN	WILD MALLARD
WHITTLER	WIGGLER	WILDNESS
WHIZZ BANG	WIGGLETTE	WILD 'N FREE
WHIZZER	WIGGLING WENCH	WILD NOBLE
WHO CARES	WIGWAM	WILD OATS
WHO DUN IT	WIG WAG	WILD ONE
WHODUNNIT	WIKIUP	WILD REVENGE
WHO KARES	WIKI WIKI	WILD ROVER
WHOLESOME GAL	WIKIWIN	WILD THING
WHOLE WORLD	WILD ABANDON	WILD TUSH
WHOLISTIC	WILD ANIMAL	WILD TURKEY
WHOOPER	WILD ANTICIPATION	WILD WARRIOR
WHOPPER STOPPER	WILD AFFAIR	WILD WEST RIDER
WHORTA WIND	WILD BEAST	WILD WHIM
WHO YOU	WILD CARD	WILD WIND

WILD _____	WIND DANCE	WINDRUSH
WILHELMINA	WIND DANCER	WIND SAFARI
WILLIAM H. ALBURY	WINDERMERE	WINDS GLOW
WILLIAM TELL	WIND DRIVEN	WINDSCAPE
WILLIN'	WIND DRIVER	WIND SHADOW
WILLING 'N ABLE	WINDFALL	WIND SLAVE
WILLIWAW	WIND FEVER	WINDS LOVER
WILLOUGHBY	WINDFLOWER	WINDS MAGIC
WILLOW	WIND FLUTE	WINDS MANTRA
WILLOWAY	WIND HEELER	WINDS MISTRESS
WILL O.	WIND HO	WIND SOCK
WILL O' WISP	WIND IMAGE	WINDSONG
WILLOWS WIND	WIND INSTRUMENT	WIND SONG
WILLOWY	WINDJAMMER	WINDSPIEL
WILL POWER	WIND JAMMER	WIND SPINNER
WILL YA	WIND KIND	WINDSPINNER
WILL WE	WINDLAND	WIND SPIRIT

More Maldivian names: SAMAASA (joke), SAMSAA (spoon), SAMUGA (compass), SARIE (trial), SEKU (silly), SIHAATU (healthy), SIKONDI (brain), SIRU (secret), SITI (letter), SITI URA (envelope), SOI (signature), SURA (image), SUTA (cigar), SUVAALU (question), SUVARUGE (heaven), SVAALU (question), UBATI (candle), UDARES (horizon), UDU (sky), UFAA (happy), ULA (bracelet), ULENI (to live), UMID KURANI (to desire), UMURU (age), UNDAGU (to annoy), UNDORLI (hammock), URA (glove), VA (round), VAADA JEHANI (to race), VAARUTA (inheritance), VAAVU (island), VAKEELU (lawyer), VALI (knife), VARA BARA (very fast), VARA GADA (very well), VA RANGALU (good wind), VARA RITI (very nice), VARA UFAA (very happy), VARIHAMA (okay), VARIVE (divorce), VELAA (turtle), VENG (eel), and VISAARE DUNI (rainbow).

WILLY WISPE	WIND LASS	WIND SPRINTER
WIL POWER	WINDLASS	WINDS STARLET
WIL TING	WIND LEGEND	WIND STALKER
WIMPLE	WIND MACHINE	WINDSTAR
WIMP 'N NERD	WIND MIGRATOR	WINDS VISA
WIMPY	WIND 'N WILLOWS	WINDS WARRIOR
WIN ALL	WINDOW PANE	WIND SWEPT
WINDALIER	WIND PIPER	WINDSWEPT
WINDBAIRN	WINDPOWERED	WINDS WIZARD
WINDBARIN	WIND PUPPY	WIND TEMPLE
WIND BARON	WIND RANGER	WINDTHIEF
WIND BLOWN	WINDRIFTER	WIND TREK
WINDBORNE	WINDQUEST	WINDUP TOY
WIND CATCHER	WIND RIDER	WIND VEHICLE
WIND CHARIOT	WIND REALM	WINDWALKER
WIND CHASER	WINDROSE	WINDWARD
WIND CHILD	WIND RUNNER	CONSPIRACY

WINDWARD LEG
WINDWARD PASSAGE
WINDWATCH
WIND WHORE
WIND WIZARD
WIND WOLF
WIND WORD
WINDY
WINDY AFFAIR
WINDY CITY
WINDY DAZE
WINDY NYMPH
WINDY RIDE
WINDY SHIP
WINDY WORLD
WIND _____
_____ WIND
WINEE PEG

WINNING BID
WINNING EDGE
WINNING POINT
WINNINGS
WINO
WINSELN
WINSLOW
WINSOM
WIN SPEPT
WINTER GHOST
WINTERHAWK
WINTERIZED
WINTER SOLSTICE
WINWANWON
WIPE OUT
WIPER OUTER
WIPPE
WIRE LESS

WITCHERY
WITCHING
WITCH O' ENDOR
WITCH OF TOWER
    BANK
WITCH'S FLOWER
WITH A LITTLE LUCK
WITHE
WITICISM
WIT 'N MITE
WITTIEST
WITT'S END
WITTY BITTY ONE
WIT VS MITE
WIWI
WIZARD
WIZARD MERLIN
WIZARDRY

---

*Spanish names: MASALLA (on beyond), QUIEN SABE (who knows?),
RENE GADO (deny), ROJO (red), SABROSO (tasty), SALA DE MAR
(sea room), SALIDA (exit), SALUDO (greeting), SANTUARIO
(sanctuary), SELLAMA SUE (her name is Sue), SEDA (silk), SEGUIDA
(immediately), SEGURA (sure), SEGURIDAD (certainty), SIN
SEMAFORO (no traffic lights), SENSACIONAL (sensational),
SEPARADA (separated), SIEMPRE (always), SIGUE MOLESTANDO
(he's still fooling around), SIGUIENTE (next), SIMPATICA (nice),
SOBRENATURAL (supernatural), SOBRINA (niece), SOLAMENTE
(only), SOLITARIO (solitary), SOLTERO (bachelor), SOMBRA
(shadow), SONRISA (smile), SUENO (dream), SUNTUOSO
(luxurious), TAAS (wok), TAFAATU (different), and TAL VEZ (maybe).*

WINGED ARROW
WINGED LADY
WINGED PEACE
WINGED VICTORY
WING IT
WINGO-WANGO
WING'N A PRAYER
WINGS
WINGS O' WIND
WINGSPAN
WINKIE
WINNEBAGO
WINNER
WINNERS CHOICE
WINNER'S CIRCLE
WINNER'S PRIDE
WINNER WIND
WINNER WINDS

WISCONSIN
WISE 1.
WISECRACKER
WISHBONE
WISHER
WISHES
WISHES & DREAMS
WISH MAKER
WISP
WISP O' WIND
WISPY
WISTAR
WISTERIA
WIST FILLED
WITCH
WITCH CRAFT
WITCHCRAFT
WITCH DOCTOR

WIZ DOM
WIZENED
WIZZAGO
WODEN
WOEBEGONE DAZE
WOLCEN
WOLF
WOLF!
WOLF WOLF
WOLFGANG
WOLFPAC
WOLF RAM
WOLKEN BRUCH
WOLLUST
WOLVERINE
WOMAN SPIRIT
_____ WOMAN
WOMBAT

WON
WONDER
WONDERLAND
WONDER MINT
WONDERSEAS
WONDER WOMAN
WONDER Y
WON ITA
WONNIG
WON TON
WOODEN BUCKET
WOOD COCK
WOOD DUCK
WOODEN CORK
WOODEN TOY
WOODEN WONDER
WOODPECKER
WOOD PUSSY
WOODWIND

WORTHY OPPONENT
WORTHY REPUTE
WRAITH
WRANGLER
WRATH
WREN
WRENEGADE
WRENNA
WRESTLER
WRIGHT WAYS
WRITE ON
WRITHER
WUHLER
WU HSIN
WUNDER
WUNDER BEAR
WUNDERLICHER
WURDE
WURF

X

"X"
X ACTA
X AMIN
X AMS
XANADU
XANTHIPPE
XARIFA
XAVIER
X AXIS
X CALIBER

More Spanish names are: TAMBIEN (also), TAMBOR (drum), TAN PRONTO COMA (as soon as), TANTA (so), TANTE (aunt), TANZIN (dancer), TALU DANDI (key), TAPFER (heroic), TARDAR (take a long time), TAREA (task), TARI (star), TASHI REETI (beautiful dish), TATER (perpetrator), TAXISTA (taxicab driver), TE (wet), TECNICA (technical), TEDU (straight), TEDUVE (get up), TEDUVERI (innocent), TEJAS (Texas), TEMA MAR (sea theme), TEMBLAR (tremble), TENER DE TODO (have everything), TENER PRISA (be in a hurry), TENER SUENO (be dreaming), TENTATIVA (attempt), TEO (oil), TERAS (glue), TESORO (treasure), TIA (aunt), TIEMPO (time), TILA (blade), and TINORS (needle).

WOODWINDS
WOOD WORK
WOODY
WOODY NOTES
WOOF WOOF
WOO HA
WOOKIE
WOOLY BEAR
WOOLY BULLY
WOO ME
WORK'A ART
WORKER BEE
WORKIN' GIRL
WORKIN' IT OUT
WORK STATION
WORLD APART
WORLDLY
WORRYSOME
WORTHY O

WUT
WYNDHAM
WYETH
WYNOT
WY NOT
WYNSONG
WYNTJE
WYOMING
WY VERN

X CEPTIONAL
X CHROMOSOME
X-CITATION
X D
XEBEC
XED
XEMA
XEN
XENIA
XENIC
XENOGENIC
XENON
XENOPHILE
XENOPHOBIA
XERES
XEROX
XEROX COPY
XERXES
XHOSA

X L
XMAL
XMAS ROSE
X NYMPHANT
XOCHIPILLI
X PAIR AMINT

X TENSION
X TERMINATOR
X TINGUISHER
X TORT
XTRA
X TRA FLASH

XYLOGRAPHY
XYLOPHILOUS
X Y Z

X PRESS
XPUHIL
X RAY
X S
X STRAHLEN
XTASEA

XTRA FIVE
XTRA HOT
X TRA NICE
X TRA RARE
XTRA _____
XYLEM

Y

YACHTING WORLD
YAHOO
YAKETY YAK

OTHER LANGUAGE SOURCES & JARGON

YAK SHA MAUCH
YANK
YANKEE
YANKEE BELL
YANKEE BELLE
YANKEE DOODLE
YANKEE TRADER
YANKEE _____
YANQUI
YAPOCK
YARROW
YAWARRA
YAWNER
YAZOO
YEAH
YEALMEGA
YEARN FOR WIND

YELP FER JOY
YELP FOR WIND
YENSHEE
YENTA
YER QUESTION
YES
YES M
YESTERDAY
YESTER DAZE
YGNACIO
YIN
YIN & YANG
YIPPIE
YMIR
YODA
YODELER
YODO

YOUNKER
YOUTH
YOUTH FILLED LUST
YOUTHFUL LADY
YOUTHFUL TYCOON
YOUTHS PASHUN
YOU TOO
YOU TWO
YOU WHO?
YOUSHITANREI
YOUNG AMERICA
YOUNG GIRL
YOUNG LOVE
YOUNG LUST
YOUR ASS
YOUR TURN
YO YO

---

*Still more Spanish: **TOCAR MI TIMBRE** (ring my bell), **TONTO** (silly), **TORMENTA** (storm), **TORTUGA** (turtle), **TRANQUILO** (calm), **TRANSITADO** (busy), **TRATAR** (treat), **TREU** (loyal), **TRES EN TRES** (3 by 3), **TRIGUENA** (brunette), **TRONAR** (thunder), **TUNU** (sharp), **TURISTA** (tourist), **ULTIMO** (latest), **UNA** (1), **UNA MAR** (sea nail), **UNICA** (only), **UNIR** (unite), **UNOS** (some), **UNTIL** (useful), **VAINA** (pod), **VAMOS** (let's go), **VEME A MI** (look at me), **VERANO** (summer), **VERDAD** (truth), **VIAJERO** (traveler), **VIENTO** (wind), **VIRGEN** (virgin), **VIRTUD** (virtue), **VISITA** (visitor), **VISTA MAR** (ocean view), **VIVA** (lively), **VOLAR** (fly), **VOLVER LOCO** (drive crazy), **VOLVERSE LOCO** (go crazy), **ZOCALO** (town square), and **ZONA** (zone).*

YEGGOWAN
YELLING
YELLO ROSE
YELLOW BIRD
YELLOW FEVER
YELLOW FIN
YELLOWFINGER
YELLOW JACKET
YELLOW PINES
YELLOW ROSE
YELLOW ROSE OF
  TEXAS
YELLOW SILK
YELLOWSTONE
YELLOW SUBMARINE
YELLOWTAIL
YELLO YAWL

YOGA
YOGI
YOKE A FLIGHT
YOKE A LOVE
YOKEL
YONALEE
YONDER
YONDER WEGO
YOOHOO
YORK
YORKSHIRE BELLE
YORKTOWN
YOSEMITE
YOU BET
YOU II
YOUNG DUCK
YOUNG TURK

YSAS
YUAN FEN
YUCATAN
YUGA
YUJUTSU
YUKON JACK
YULE LOG
YULE TIDE
YULINDA
YUMMY
YUM YUM
YUPPIE
YUPPIE GUPPIE
YURS TRU LE
YURS TRU LY
Y YORKER

Z

"Z"
ZACH
ZACKEN
ZADOR
ZAG
ZAHLBAR
ZAHRA
ZAIDA
Z AIR
ZALEK

ZAUBER
ZAUBERIN
ZAU ZAU
ZA-ZEN
Z BOAT
ZEAL
ZEALOUS
ZEBRA
ZEBU
ZEE BOAT
ZEE BOOST
ZEE GLE
ZEE LOVER
ZEE WIFE
ZEE WOMAN
ZEICHEN
ZEITGEIST
ZEITLEBENS
ZENITH

ZIGGY
ZIG ZAG
ZILLAH
ZIMPLE MATTA
ZIMPLE SOLU SHUN
ZIMPLE ZIMON
ZINC
ZING
ZINGARA
ZINGER
ZINK
ZINNO
ZIN ZA SCHUN
ZIP
ZIPADEE DOODA
ZIP A DEE DOO DA
ZIP A LONG
ZIP CODE
ZIP GUN

---

*Chinese: **SHIH SHIH WU** (net of jewels), **TUN WU** (flash of insight), **WU-HSIN** (true mind), and **YUAN FEN** (people and objects meet not by chance but because of destiny; and by so meeting, enrich one another).*

*Greek: **DAEMON** (guardian spirit), **DELPHIN** (dolphin), **HELIOS** (sun), **KAIROS** (devine time), **OIJOS** (house), **SARX** (flesh), **SKORPIOS** (scorpion), and **THERMOS** (hot).*

*Sanskrit: **AMIDA** (infinate life), **RAJAS** (activity, desire), **SAHA** (endurance), **SATVA** (harmony, rhythm), **SVAAP** (dream), and **VEDA** (knowledge).*

ZANAHORIA
ZANDER
ZANKISCH
ZANNY
ZANY
ZANZIBAR
ZAP
ZAPATA
ZAPATO
ZAPFCHEN
ZAPOTEC
ZAPPA
ZAPPEL
ZARAGOZA
ZART MADCHEN
ZARTLICH
ZATTA WAY
ZATS ALL FOLKS
ZAT WAY

ZEN
ZEN MONK
ZENO
ZEPHER
ZEPHYR
ZEPHYRUS
ZEPPELIN
ZER
ZERO
ZERRBILD
ZEST
ZESTY
ZESTY _____
ZETA
ZEUS
ZEVENTY FI
ZIA
ZIG
ZIGGURAT

ZIPPITY DOO DAH
ZIPPORAH
ZIPPY
ZIREN
ZISE WAY
ZIT
ZITHER
ZLING
ZOAVE
ZOCALO
ZODIAC
ZOFE
ZOLA
ZONA
ZONED
ZONE TORRID
ZOO
_____ ZOO
ZOO CREW

ZOO ILLOGICAL
ZOOKEY   _____
ZOOM
ZORN   _____
ZORO
ZORRO   _____
ZOROASTER
ZO ZO   _____
Z ROW
Z SEA   _____ .
ZU
ZUCHTHENGST   _____
ZUCHTIG
ZUCKEN   _____
ZUG
ZUGABE   _____
ZUGELLOS
ZUGLEICH   _____
ZUGVOGEL   _____

---

*Italian: **BEN TROVATO** (well-found), **DOLCE FAR NIENTE** (sweet idleness), **IL PENSIEROSO** (the pensive man), **L'ALLEGRO** (merry man), **SCAPPARE** (to flee), and **VINDICTA** (vengeance).*

*Proper names may vary slightly according to their Latin (L), French (F), Italian (I), Spanish (S), or Greek (G) spellings: **FLORENCE, FLORENTIA (L), FLORENECE (F), FIORENZA (I), FLORENCIA (S),** or **FLORENTIA (G); AMADEUS, AMADEUS (L), AMEDEE (F), AMEDEO (I),** or **AMADEO (S);** and **HENRY, HENRICUS (L), HENRI (F), ENRICO (I), ENRIQUE (S),** or **HEINRICH (G).***

ZULANE
ZULU   _____
ZUNDEN
ZUNI   _____
ZUSTANDE
ZUVIEL
ZWECK   _____
ZWILLING
ZWINKERN   _____
ZYDECO
ZYNIKER
ZYPRESSE
Z ZEBRA   _____
ZZZ
ZZZIP   _____

_____ _____

_____ _____

_____ _____

_____ _____

_____ _____

_____ _____

_____ _____

_____ _____

_____ _____

_____ _____

_____ _____

_____ _____

_____

A variety of other languages have contributed these boat names:
***BAIDARKA** (Aleutian: kayak),* ***DAKHALA** (Arabic: sanctuary),* ***IA
ORANA** (Tahitian: welcome),* ***JUMBIE** (West Indian: ghost),* ***JA**
(Swedish: yes),* ***MARESIA** (Portuguese: sea spray),* ***QUETZALOCOATI**
(Aztec: feathered spirit),* ***RAWHA** (Lite: wilderness),* ***SAMIZDAT**
(Russian: self-published),* ***SEHANS** (Dutch: small fort),* ***SEKET**
(Egyptian Goddess of Magic),* ***SOINTY** (Finnish: harmony & balance),*
***TALOFA** (Samoan: hello),* ***TANE** (Thaitian: man),* ***UKAZ** (Russian:
edict),* ***UGGR** (Norse: fear),* ***VAHINE** and **WAHINE** (Tahitian: woman).*

_____ _____

_____ _____

_____ _____

_____ _____

_____ _____

_____ _____

_____ _____

_____ _____

_____ _____

_____ _____

INDEX

INDEX

speed, 97, 110
sport, 105, 108
sporting interests 57, 58, 76
stars, 28, 35
stage, 35
streamlined craft, 30, 97
subtle, to throw opponents off guard, 104
sun, 82
super-achievers, 59
superstition, 7

T
television, 35
tenders, 90-91
The Bible, 25
threatening, to intimidate opponents, 101
toasts, 77
track racing, 108
trade names, 75
tradition, 7, 32
translation guides, 120
trees, 79
trimarans, 94
TV, 35

U
unexpected meaning, 14, 23, 120
utopian, 29

V
vanity license plates, 111
variations, 16
vessel's intended use, 69

W
water skiers, 43, 98, 100, 101, 103
windjammers, 9
wind terms, 83, 84
witchery, 86
"witches' winds", 84
word substitution, 60, 114, 115
wrecks, 89
why a name like that?, 4, 23

Z
zodiac, signs of, 28

John Corcoran has sailed and skippered 11 boats, has restored a classic staysail racing schooner, and has built three sailboats. John has 30 years of experience "messing about in boats" and is currently planning a solo circumnavigation.

This book was originally John's idea. He had accumulated a large number of interesting and humorous boat names as he cruised far and wide, and his literary interests prompted the idea to share these names with others. He has published a number of articles on social issues, and is a published poet.

John, a longtime resident of the Pacific region, now resides in a wooded Virginia glen far from tidal influence while writing and studying hull design.

Lew Hackler has owned some 16 boats including a 40-foot double cabin motoryacht: FAIR DINKUM, (Aussie slang) which he named and lived aboard for ten years, following an extended stay in Australia. Other boats have included a 16-foot ski boat: QUITS, (it had a cantankerous 22 HP outboard motor); a 26-foot sloop: A OVER T (British slang, again influenced by an overseas visit); a 41-foot motorsailer: SEA STAR, which he lived aboard (named for the 5-pointed starfish found in southern waters); and his current 30-foot sailing sloop: SEASTAR II, which has two dinghies: SEA BISCUIT (an inflatable), and STAR FISH (a hardshell), with which he cruises the Chesapeake Bay, south Atlantic coast, Florida Keys, and Bahamas.

Lew is author of THE COMPLETE SAILOR'S LOG, and co-author of the more recent SENSIBLE CRUISING: THE THOREAU APPROACH, which received excellent reviews and was a Book-of-the-Month Dolphin selection with record sales.